BRISTOL & CO

HELEN REID

First published in 1987 by
Redcliffe Press Ltd, 49 Park Street, Bristol 1

ISBN 0 948265 61 2

*Typeset and printed in Great Britain by
Penwell Ltd, Parkwood, Callington, Cornwall*

Contents

Bristol Bridge, Bristol's prime medieval shopping centre.

Introduction

This book is a celebration of survivors. No other provincial city in the country can boast more than 130 firms which are over a century and in some cases two centuries old. (There may be more which I have failed to trace – if so, my apologies to them.)

Any firm which has lasted this long has survived fantastic changes, from copperplate to computers, from horse-and-cart to Concorde. During the last century, these firms have seen the arrival of the telephone, the typewriter, electricity, the motor car, radio and television, the vote and the sewing machine. They have survived two world wars and two major recessions, and the older firms lived through the American War of Independence, the Napoleonic Wars, and the abolition of slavery; three events which had a powerful effect on Bristol's import and export trade. They have also survived in a world of take-overs, many of them with the same family in charge. A century ago, with large Victorian families, it was easy to find a son to take over the business, but nowadays with small families and a much wider choice of employment, finding a successor is much harder. Some of the firms in this book have sadly reached the end of the family line, after three, four and five generations, and there is no son or daughter to take over.

Many of the firms have changed ownership, but I have included, with a few exceptions, only those which have retained their original names. Also outside the scope of this book are the equally old schools, charities, public houses and branches of banks, building societies and insurance companies.

In no sense is this a list of company histories. I have tried to give an idea of what these firms were like when they were founded, and who their founders were, and to show how they adapted to changing times and consumer demands.

How many will survive into the next century is questionable; during the course of writing, six firms closed down and more were taken over. In the last two decades alone some 40 other old firms have gone under, taking a large slice of Bristol's history with them.

One clear message has emerged from writing this book. Vital social history is locked away in the archives of these venerable firms, and it is a tragedy that so many, whether through the Blitz, through moving premises, or being taken over, have lost irreplaceable records of the way they were a century or more ago. More than a dozen firms, one or two dating back to the 18th century, could tell me absolutely nothing about their history, because their records had been lost or destroyed. A few hours a year spent on a scrapbook would have made future historians happy!

My thanks must go to the many firms who spent time telling me family stories, hunting for old photographs, and delving in dusty records, and to the company archivists who allowed me to quote from their work. Also invaluable have been the street directories and local archives in Bristol Reference Library, and, of course, the Annals of John Latimer. Thanks are also due to Bristol United Press for photographs.

Finally, thanks to R. Marleyn for advice, suggestions and support.

The Old Dutch House, bombed in the Second World War, seen in the Edwardian period, with Jones department store on the left. Note the milk delivery cart.

1 – "Trade, mighty trade here holds resistless sway."

Richard Savage, 1742.

From the 15th century onwards, Bristol was famous as a trading city: every visitor remarked on it, often in distinctly unflattering terms. Walpole called the city "the dirtiest great shop I ever saw", Defoe said the souls of Bristolians were "engrossed with lucre". Chatterton predictably attacked the city for being mercenary: "Lost to all learning, elegance and sense, long had this famous city told her pence".

From Saxon times, Bristol's geography had made her prosperous. Her good sea and road links, a natural harbour (improved as early as the 13th century) and her trade-mad citizens gave Bristol a head start over her rivals. By the medieval period there was a flourishing port trade in wine, timber, fish, leather, tin and wool, and a distribution system for imports into Wales, the West Country and south-east England.

The merchants turned retailers, too, selling from warehouses to the public, as did the craftsmen, who sold their products from their homes.

The first shops were established in the houses on Bristol Bridge, the prime site. Others were set up in High Street, Corn Street, Wine Street and Broad Street, which intersected the medieval heart of the city, making it a clearly defined shopping centre by the 14th century. Occupations clustered together: jewellers and mercers on Bristol Bridge, wool drapers in the High Street, linen drapers in Wine Street. Temple Gate became the area for butchers, while the merchants who used the port traded on the waterfronts.

But most people shopped in markets and at fairs, and also bought from hawkers in the streets, and this remained true for the poorer citizens up to the end of the Victorian period. The markets each had a defined trade; one for meat, one for vegetables, one for livestock and one for poultry, while non-perishable items would be bought at annual fairs or from travelling pedlars.

The idea of retailing in the modern sense did not really arrive until the end of the 18th century, when there was a revolution: shopkeepers began to make a living by selling not their own but other people's goods, and they stopped specialising in one line. So you find Alex Jolly of the Hotwells selling in 1775 perfume, confectionery and snuff. The Hotwell visitors prompted Bristol's first purpose-built shops, and this tourist trade led to the development of the first suburban shopping area in Clifton.

The railways brought another major change in retailing; the cheap products of the Industrial Revolution could now be distributed far more easily, and shops began to carry a much wider range; this led to men like Thomas Jones of Wine Street opening up his department store in 1843. With shops like this, who needed St James' Fair, an event whose fame had spread even as far as Moscow? By 1838, it had become a sideshow, the 19th century equivalent of a pop festival, and it was abolished. Next came a proper system of public transport, which changed the pattern of central and suburban shopping; with a more mobile population, traders began to compete fiercely, and to cut prices and advertise.

By modern standards, Victorian Bristol was vastly overshopped; a street like East Street, Bedminster, or the Hotwell Road would have ten butchers, five bakers, eight greengrocers, and so on. They survived because poverty, lack of refrigeration and cooking facilities made daily shopping necessary, while the better-off Victorians were dedicated consumers, over-eating and over- dressing.

The puzzle is why the 130 firms in this book should have survived while thousands failed. Bristol was once famous for wool, glass, brass, china, soap, sugar, pins, cotton, leather and coal. All these industries have vanished. Yet other old industries have survived and prospered: wine, timber, cocoa, tobacco, printing and shipping, all survive even though the port which was the reason for their founding in Bristol is no longer a factor.

Food and drink, the most basic commodities of all, are trades with few survivors, yet the carriers, who should have been wiped out by the coming of the railways and motor transport, have adapted and survived. Jewellers and solicitors seem to have great staying power. Some firms have had to diversify furiously to stay in business, while others are still selling exactly the same items, a century or more later. A few have flourished in symbiotic relationships, being set up to serve another industry, as Mardons and Robinsons were for Wills, and for the retail trade.

It is mainly the firms which have not been affected by the multiple-chain, superstore style trading that survive best, but another explanation must be Bristol's tradition of protectionism. It began with the medieval guilds which, with the aid of the Corporation, exercised huge power over craftsmen and shopkeepers, dictating what goods they could sell, whom they could employ, the days and hours when they could trade; they even made rules about the number of tallow candles that could be burned at night. Only burgesses and freemen could trade in the city. This status was achieved only by birth, marriage or the completion of a long apprenticeship. "Foreigners", that is non- Bristolians, were simply not allowed to trade, and there were huge penalties if they were caught selling goods or supplying shops in the city. In 1652 the Merchant Venturers appointed a man at £10 a year "to search out those who shall buy and sell strangers' goods contrary to the privileges of the city, and inform the Sheriff of his proceedings, to the end that such goods may be seized as foreign bought and foreign sold". The fines were enormous: £5 a day, or £20 on each occasion, and goods seized. You could say Bristol was a pioneer in restrictive practices! Monopolies were rife; there were ordinances preventing butchers from selling cooked meat, thus protecting inn-keepers; no one but an inn-keeper could stable horses, joiners could not supply locks, and so on. Every trade had a network of monopolies and restrictions.

This was true of all cities up to the end of the 17th century, but Bristol kept protectionism going, in spirit if not in letter, with far greater vigour than most: Defoe remarked in the 1720s that the city could have been double its size if it had not been for "the tenacious folly of its inhabitants" and "corporation-tyranny". The 1832 Reform Bill, passed at last largely because of the terror inspired by the Bristol Riots, gave far more men the vote, and so made them freemen, ending the whole concept of "foreigners" in Bristol. The Municipal Act of 1835 made it legal for anyone to trade anywhere. But the spirit of protectionism lingered on – and perhaps it still does. Bristol likes to look after its own.

And there is an interesting feminist footnote: the restrictive practices did not extend towards Bristol's freewomen who, up to Victorian times, followed an amazing variety of occupations. Late 18th century street directories show 93 different trades being carried

A busy scene in Castle Street in 1930s. The entire street was demolished in the Blitz.

on by women, including plasterer, gardener, plumber, blacksmith, watchmaker, butcher, wheelwright, tiler, harpsichord builder, timber dealer and inn-keeper. A century later, when the population of the city had almost trebled, only 40 different and more feminine trades, such as mantle-making and millinery, appear. Presumably propriety had driven out the rest.

2 – "Industrious, obliging, upright and punctual."

This was how William Mathews described the traders of Bristol in his *Complete Guide* of 1793. So what were the shops like, and what were conditions like for those working in them?

The earliest businesses were started in private houses; a merchant or shopkeeper would trade from the ground floor and live above. Some shops were built-on lean-tos, and all would be open to the weather unless the trader was very rich and could afford glass – as jewellers usually could. A wooden lattice would be put up at night to protect the goods from burglars. This type of shop lasted well into the 18th century: Poet Laureate Robert Southey recollected that his draper father had worked in an open shop in Wine Street in 1760, and Latimer claims there were still some as late as the 1820s. Reminders of the open shop are the few greengrocers', butchers' and fishmongers' shops which still have shutters rather than glass windows.

By the 18th century, the purpose-built shop had arrived. The earliest example seems to be the Colonnade in Hotwells, a half-crescent of houses built in 1786 with shops on the ground floor, which had larger windows. These shops sold trinkets to visitors to the Hotwell. The Upper and Lower Arcades (1824) in Broadmead were next, and from then on it became common to build a rank of houses with shops underneath – the grandest was the Royal Promenade built in 1860 in Queen's Road. And between these dates, hundreds of Georgian houses had converted ground floors. Park Street was originally entirely private houses, and the last vestige can be seen at No. 51, which still has its steps and front door intact.

Plate-glass windows did not come in until the 19th century, and with them came the new art of window dressing and the new trade of shop-fitting.

In 1820, William Parnall started trading in a cellar in Narrow Wine Street, making weights and measures, and later branching out into other shop-keeping equipment: scale pans, tea bins, canisters and scoops. The weighing machines and the shop fittings became two distinct businesses, and by the 1880s, **Parnalls** was the biggest shopfitting firm in the country, with branches in London and Swansea, warehouses and showrooms in Narrow Wine Street, a scale works at Fishponds and a showroom in Fairfax Street for shop fittings. They fitted out shops in London as well as the West and supplied "the latest novelties and improvements – scoops, barrows, counter boxes, tills, tickets, window name plates, tobacco cutters, bottling machines, beer engines, hand carts, coffee mills, tea mixers, hoists and lifts." For butchers they even supplied sawdust: "There is hardly a city or town in Great Britain where their productions are not known and appreciated", said a description in the 1890s. They had ten representatives on the road and employed 400 workmen, and in 1889 went into shop-fronts as well, providing: architectural ironwork, iron and glass canopies, gates and railings and display units. In 1899 they became associated with W. and T. Avery, and the manufacture of weighing machines was phased out in favour of shop-fitting. In the 1914-18 war, their workshops were used to produce 600 aeroplanes and seaplanes.

They moved to their present home in Fishponds in 1923 and supplied a new generation of shopfronts, with lobbies and island windows. Famous contracts at the time were for the bronze shopfronts and display cases in Piccadilly Circus Underground Station and the stainless steel canopies at the Savoy Hotel and the Shakespeare Memorial Theatre at Stratford-on-Avon.

They also did extensive work for the Co-op, Liptons, Sainsbury's and Selfridges, from the turn of the century. Between the wars they started making and fitting cold storage units and refrigerated display units. The Second World War brought a return to aircraft work – Parnalls made airframe components and fuselage sections in metal and wood for famous marques from the Tiger Moth to the Horsa glider, and the work continued in peacetime with the interior finishing of the Britannia aircraft, exploiting the use of a new material, plastic. In the late Forties, they began catering for the new shopping fashion, the supermarket, and developed metal shelving and display units. Parnalls postwar has had contracts at the best addresses: 10 Downing Street, Buckingham Palace, the Houses of Parliament and the QE2.

As the population of Victorian Bristol expanded and the building boom began, certain streets became more important as shopping areas, and the merchant traders in the centre of the city began to move their homes and businesses out to the edges of the city, leaving the waterfront areas free for entirely commercial development. Park Street, Whiteladies Road, Stokes Croft, Gloucester Road, East Street and North Street, Bedminster, all became clearly defined as shopping streets.

Shop signs had persisted as an aid for the illiterate until 1770, although they had been banned by the Corporation as early as 1749, because of their danger to passers-by. The signs, a golden boy for a jeweller, a wig and griffin for a barber, a bible for a bookseller, a coffin shroud for the undertaker and a half moon and wheatsheaf for a draper, all disappeared – now we have only the striped pole of the barber and the three balls sign of the pawnbroker to remind us.

In medieval times, a merchant would store his wares in his own house, or in cellars nearby, but as businesses got bigger, they needed a warehouse, and providing this storage space became a trade.

Ford and Canning are the third oldest firm to be featured in this book: their business started in King Street Hall, near the modern King Street, in 1712, when Alexander Ford was apprenticed to wine cooper John Rainstorp. Ford took over the business in 1749, paying £1,475 for it at auction, and worked as a cooper. His widow and stepson William Ford inherited the business and built a warehouse in 1777, and presumably stored wine, since in 1810 they were still working as coopers to the wine trade. They built another warehouse in 1830, and traded from then on as merchants. During the Bristol Riots, they had their property protected by James Ford, who was made a special constable at the age of 18 and who had a trusted band of men with bar shot to throw on the rioters' heads, should they try to break in and start looting.

Thomas Canning joined the firm in 1850, when the main function was clearly warehousing, mostly of tobacco. A brochure for 1878 shows that they charged 15s. a year as rent per hogshead of tobacco, and for hogsheads in transit, 3d. a week, and there were various rates for snuff in barrels, cigars, and cases of cut tobacco. Later literature proves that they owned a dried fruit warehouse, a "free" warehouse for general goods,

SHOP FITTINGS AND REQUISITES

Of every description, for all Trades.

GROCERS'	BUTCHERS'	CONFECTIONERS'	HOTEL BARS
Balances	Scales	Glasses	Beer Engines
Canisters	Cutlery	Show Stands	Spirit Casks
Coffee Mills	Sausage Machines	Brackets	Mullers
Tea Mills	Fillers	Urns	Measures
Fruit Cleaners	Brine Pumps	Whisks	Taps, Pumps
Counters	Skewers	Marble Tables	Cork Drawers
Show Cases	Seasonings	Suspenders	Bottling Machines

And every Trade Requisite.   *Price Lists on application.*

Address in Full. } **PARNALL & SONS, LTD.** { The Old Firm.

The largest Complete Shop Fitters in the Kingdom,

NARROW WINE STREET, BRISTOL;

Telephone No. 356.   And at London and Swansea.   Telegrams—"Parnall, Bristol."

An 1897 advertisement showing the huge range of shop-fitting accessories that Parnall & Sons supplied to Bristol firms.

FORD'S TOBACCO WAREHOUSES,
KING STREET HALL, BRISTOL.

CONSOLIDATED RATES
ON DIRECT IMPORTATIONS.

RECEIVING *ex* SHIP, Weighing Nett, Sampling, Coopering, Marking, Housing, and Rent for 12 months ; due on the delivery of the Weighing Account.

HOGSHEADS AND TIERCES 9 cwt. and over, gross				...	15/-	each.
Do. do. under 9 cwt.. gross				...	12/-	,,
BALES and CASES, not exceeding 1½ cwt.				...	3/3	,,
,,	,,	,,	,, 2 ,,	...	4/3	,,
,,	,,	,,	,, 3 ,,	...	5/3	,,
,,	,,	,,	,, 4 ,,	...	6/3	,,
,,	,,	,,	,, 5 ,,	...	7/3	,,

over 5 cwt. in the same proportion.

CIGARS.—Swiss, in ordinary sized packages	...	4/-	,,
,, Continental, American, (in cases of) Havannah, and Manilla (10,000 each)	...	7/6	,,
In larger cases	...minimum	10/-	each.
CAVENDISH AND CUT TOBACCO—Cases		4/6	,,
,, ,, ,, Boxes		3/6	,,

Special Rates for any extraordinary sizes.

RENT

On Direct Importations in second, and subsequent years ; and on Removals, Coastwise, or Inland, from date of arrival.

HOGSHEADS AND TIERCES 9 cwt. and over, gross,	6/6	each.
TIERCES AND HOGSHEADS under 9 cwt. gross	5/-	,,
BALES AND CASES, not exceeding 2 cwt. ...	3/-	,,
,, over ,, ...	5/-	,,
CIGARS—Swiss in ordinary sized packets	3/-	,,
All others	6/6	,,
CAVENDISH & CUT TOBACCO—Cases	3/-	,,
,, Boxes	2/6	,,

} Per year or any portion thereof

PACKAGE RENT,
For Goods in transit for Home-Ports only.

HOGSHEADS (as above)	per week	3d.	each.
TIERCES (as above)	,,	2d.	,,
BALES & CASES, not exceeding 2 cwt.	,,	2d.	,,
,, ,, over 2 cwt.	,,	3d.	,,
CAVENDISH—			
Boxes and Cases	,,	1d.	,,
Kegs and Tierces	,,	2d.	,,
CUT TOBACCO—			
Cases, not exceeding 1 cwt.	,,	1d.	,,
,, ,, over 1 cwt.	,,	2d.	,,
CIGARS AND CHEROOTS.—			
Cases, containing not more than 10,000 ...	,,	3d.	,,
,, ,, ,, 15,000 ...	,,	4d.	,,
,, ,, ,, 20,000 ...	,,	6d.	,,
Snuff in Barrels or Cases ... per cwt.	,,	1d.	

Storing other firms' goods was big business for Ford & Canning, Warehousemen, as this 1879 price list shows.

and several bonded warehouses for tobacco, wines and spirits. "All empties are the property of the tobacco cooper," said a leaflet, showing the old connection between coopering and warehousing still existed.

Part of the warehousing was destroyed by the Blitz, along with most of the company's records. The firm built anew near the old site, in Canon's Marsh where they now specialise in storage and distribution.

Until the end of the 18th century, shops were mainly run by the families who owned them, but with the Industrial Revolution and the huge increase in retailing, shop assistants were needed, and a new servitude began.

Shop workers nowadays would find the hours their Victorian counterparts worked intolerable. A sixteen hour day was common, and when the shops closed, there was cleaning up and window dressing to do. The average working week was 85 hours.

While young factory workers had their hours limited by an Act of 1847, it took until this century to pass a bill limiting the hours of shopworkers, and compelling early closing one day a week. The battle went on from the 1840s to 1911; Bank Holidays were achieved in 1871, paid holidays in the 1930s. There was no regulation of pay either; the Truck Act of 1831, which insisted wages had to be paid in cash and not kind, did not apply to shop workers. Since the assistants usually lived-in, their employers were able to exploit them by paying them with bed and board (often with more than one person to a bed and very bad board) plus a pittance in wages. They also had their staff on tap all the hours they wanted. Bristol M.P., A.B. Winterbotham in 1891 gave evidence in the House when an attempt was being made to establish early closing on Saturdays; he spoke of shops in Bristol opening for 80 or 90 hours a week. But there was also an exception in Bristol: Samuel Budgett the wholesale grocer was a pioneer in early closing, giving his staff time off on Saturdays as early as 1851.

The reason for the long, late hours was the fierce and bitter competition: Victorian Bristol was greatly over-shopped and the ones which stayed open latest got the most trade. So shop-keepers would start spying on the competition at around 9 p.m. If one stayed open, the rest followed suit, and attempts to regulate shop hours were looked on as an affront to free enterprise, though the very high class shops did close earlier. The result of all this was tragic for the shop assistants, who were reckoned to be one of the most unhealthy groups of workers in the country. They suffered particularly from TB, anaemia, and backache, not surprisingly, since they were not permitted chairs to sit on when not serving. Their one day off was Sunday, and most of them were so exhausted that they stayed in bed, if their employers allowed it. Some closed the doors to the dormitories and living quarters on a Sunday from 10 a.m. to 10 p.m.

The public were urged to come to the aid of this oppressed class by asking shop owners to provide seats for the staff and by refusing to shop on Saturday afternoons, but the assistants, locked into an apprenticeship system, were apathetic about taking action which would certainly lead to dismissal; many of them planned to become shop-owners themselves and would expect their staff to work in the same way.

Their lives were made worse by hundreds of petty rules, infringement of which meant fines. Cleaning shoes in the bedroom, failing to eat the food provided, cutting cloth so that a remnant resulted all attracted fines, as did losing duplicate bills (a monstrous 5s. fine), and some shops had the infamous rule that an employee could be sacked if a customer left the shop without making a purchase.

Conditions in Bristol were just as bad as in London and other cities, judging from Government Blue Papers. The drapers were the worst offenders, often expecting their staff to work from 7.30 a.m. to 11 p.m. for wages which amounted to less than 6d. an hour. They allowed half an hour off for lunch and 15 minutes for tea.

The consciences of the do-gooding ladies of Bristol were stirred, if only from the fear that the shop workers, penned up six days a week, would be "immoral" on a Sunday.

In 1878 a group of Redland ladies, supporters of the Early Closing Movement, met and resolved: "We the undersigned, in view of the great physical and moral evils resulting to so many young men and women in the city from the practice of shops being open till the late hours, would earnestly recommend their fellow-citizens to abstain from the practice of shopping after 4 p.m. on Saturdays and after 7 p.m. on other days."

It was a vain request, for the shop-keepers realised that for the young and poor, window shopping was a form of entertainment that could lead to a sale. The better class shops closed early on a Saturday but the shops in Castle Street and Old Market stayed open late on Saturday nights right up to the Second World War.

3 – Food and Drink

"Too much in turtle Bristol's sons delight,
Too much o'er bowls of sack prolong the night"
–Lord Byron

Food and drink are the most basic commodities of all, and Bristol was always famous for its markets, where most Bristolians shopped for food until late in the last century. They also bought food – cooked pies, fruit, vegetables, fish, muffins, and so on – from hawkers. Mathews in his 1793 directory says that "all sorts of fish, vegetables and fruit, fresh butter and numerous other articles are hawked and cried daily about the streets, which are resounding from morning till night with the harsh music of mercantile orators."

He also mentions "The great plenty, variety and cheapness of provisions in the market, the profusion of vegetables fruit and flowers" and "the continual importation of poultry, pigs, excellent salt butter, eggs and fruit from adjoining counties and Wales."

The Welsh traders, strictly regulated by the Corporation to protect local interests, sold their wares on Welsh Back; by the 18th century, there was a meat, dairy, vegetable and flower market at St. Nicholas, St. James's Market in Union Street for "every sort of animal and vegetable food", Butcher's Row near Lawford's Place, a fish market in Union Street, as well as fish sold on the Back, a cheese market, a weekly cattle market, and a hay and corn market – evidence of which remain in the city's street names. There were also numerous breweries, cider manufacturers, distillers and, of course, wine merchants.

But with the growth of the Victorian suburbs, people began to live further away from the food markets, and began to have to rely on local shops, which unlike the markets, were not under the Corporation's control as far as quality went. Adulteration of food, particularly of bread, was a common problem in the first half of the 19th century. The poor had an appalling diet, not just because of their poverty but because of the adulteration of the food they could afford, often bought from stalls and cookshops because their homes had no proper cooking facilities.

It was for this reason, to provide pure food at fair prices, that the Co-operative movement began in Rochdale in 1844, and came to Bristol in 1859. Co-operation had a shaky start in the city: there were attempts to get shops going in 1859 and 1867, but the first Co-operative Society to keep a shop running was the Bedminster one, which opened in West Street in 1882.

The **Bristol and District Co-operative Society** was started by a group of trade unionists in 1884 in a shop in Houlton Street, St. Paul's. One of the co-operators was shoe-maker John Wall, who wrote a history of the Bristol Society. "We shall never forget it! The quaint shop, the small counters, the meagre supply of groceries and provisions – in all nineteen articles which had cost £20... The Committee, inexperienced yet willing, with white aprons tied on firmly, bustling around with the importance but also the love of a mother hen with her first brood."

The store opened two nights a week for its first six months; during the first quarter, average weekly trading was £10, and at the end of that time £130 had been taken and a "divi" of 1s. 6d. was handed out. Branch stores opened in St. George's Road, Hotwells, and Lawrence Hill, and the movement was on its way as the first of the chain grocery stores. By 1918, the Bristol Society was prosperous enough to acquire land in Castle Street for new central premises which finally opened as a department store in 1930. By the time the Second World War broke out, the Bristol Society's annual sales exceeded £3 million. By then the Co-op could care for Bristolians from the cradle to the grave with tailoring, barbering, chiropody, hairdressing, removals, travel, milk, bread and funeral services, and there was a strong social and educational side as well.

But the war marked a cross-roads. The department store in Castle Street was one of the few to survive the Blitz, and traded on, a lone bastion in the wasteland (as recently as 1960 it had a "Mantles" department) until Broadmead was re-developed and plans to build Fairfax House were laid. The new store marked a new era of shopping, when the customer had to go to the shop rather than the shop to the customer, and this was an alien concept for the Co-op. It took them two decades to adjust to the new supermarket and then superstore mentality. The Bristol Society ended the divi, joined the national Co-operative Wholesale Services and began a fight for customers that is still going on, as small suburban branches close to howls of protest.

The Co-op had great muscle a century ago, with its chain of branches; the small independent food retailers had to struggle against huge competition, since every suburban street could boast half a dozen butchers, bakers, grocers and greengrocers. That any of them have survived a century or more is a miracle, when you consider how difficult it is to diversify or compete against chain stores and supermarkets.

There are precious few fishmongers left in the city, let alone ones which go back a century, so **Lloyd Bros.,** of Whiteladies Road is a remarkable example. Lloyds was founded in 1865 by Gabriel Lloyd who at the tender age of 15 had to take over his father's business at the corner of Apsley Road and Whiteladies Road. Gabriel Lloyd senior had started as a costermonger, done well and bought a shop, but he died prematurely, probably from drink, and his son Gabriel, who had wanted to be an artist, had to become a fishmonger. He prospered, for he was an astute and hardworking man whose working day started at 5 a.m. in the fish market. According to his great-grandson Graham Lloyd, the fish he sold to his Victorian customers would have been fresher than the fish we can buy today: "All the catches came by rail, packed in ice, from small independent fishermen in Devon and Cornwall, before the days when catches came frozen from Hull and Grimsby," he says. The Victorians ate a lot of fish, especially on Fridays, and liked to buy cockles, mussels, eels, whelks and oysters from stalls, and prices were remarkably cheap.

Of Gabriel Lloyd's nine children, three entered the business: his daughter Daisy and sons Arnold (reluctantly) and Stanley. By 1888 there was another shop at 134 Whiteladies Road, and around 1900 Gabriel bought the present shop at No. 128 – he was a shrewd buyer of property. He was also a strict teetotaller and Wesleyan: at Christmas when the shop was festooned from the roof with poultry and game, an order of turkeys would arrive from Ireland, complete with a present: a keg full of Irish whiskey. To the utter despair of his workforce, Gabriel would ceremoniously pour the lot down the drain.

In the years before the Second World War, Arnold Lloyd had set up branches at

Late Victorian flower sellers in St Nicholas Market.

Above: Brokenbrow's elaborate letterhead of the 1920s features the coat of arms of the Fishmongers.

Below: A Harvey's advertisment of 1922, when Bristol Milk cost only £1.70 a *dozen*!

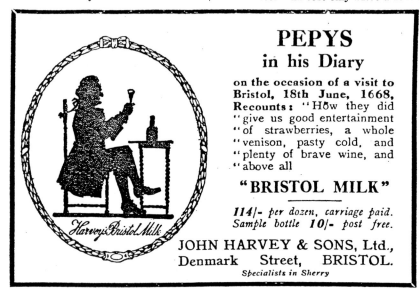

PEPYS
in his Diary

on the occasion of a visit to Bristol, 18th June, 1668, Recounts: "How they did "give us good entertainment "of strawberries, a whole "venison, pasty cold, and "plenty of brave wine, and "above all

"BRISTOL MILK"

114/- per dozen, carriage paid. Sample bottle 10/- post free.

JOHN HARVEY & SONS, Ltd.,
Denmark Street, BRISTOL.
Specialists in Sherry

Henleaze Road, and lower down at Whiteladies Gate, and these continued despite the Depression of the Thirties. Graham Lloyd joined in 1939, when the firm still had four horses and various wagons, stabled in Woodbury Lane opposite, for deliveries. "We thought nothing if a customer in Sneyd Park ordered twice a day. We delivered – even if it was a herring." During the war, famous customers arrived, because of the evacuation of the BBC from London to Bristol: Sir Adrian Boult and announcer Stuart Hibberd shopped there. After the war, when the firm became Lloyd Bros. with two cousins as directors, there was more expansion, creating seven branches, which were separated off in 1979. With a history of reluctant Lloyds taking over from their fathers, it is nice to record that in the fourth generation, Adrian Lloyd has followed his father into the business from his own choice!

One of the wholesale fishmongers whom Gabriel Lloyd would have dealt with was **William Brokenbrow** who, in 1850, set up in the fish market, then on the Quay by Bristol Bridge.

His son, James William, took over, and his son Douglas William, of the third generation, now retired, went into the firm in 1927: he remembers the Thirties when mackerel cost 4s. a stone, and cod fillet 3s. 6d. a stone, while the more expensive fish was lemon sole, at 6s. 6d. a stone.

In 1939, the day after war broke out, the fish trade was taken over by the Ministry of Food and all transport was pooled. "The result was chaos," he says. "After about three weeks we were notified that the fish distribution scheme was scrapped and that normal working could resume. The Market suffered badly from bomb and fire damage during the Blitz, but trade carried on regardless."

His wife recalls the pre-war decade when late night shopping on a Saturday was a popular entertainment in the city.

"Up to the 1939 war, the fish, fruit and meat markets kept open on Saturday nights until nine and ten o'clock, and as almost all the other shops and especially the food shops stayed open late, the area was thronged with people. Whole families would come to shop, children as well. Since there were no freezers as we know them, perishables were sold off very cheaply, so that a good supply of fish or meat could be had for a few pence. It was all very jolly, with lots of joky remarks and repartee. The markets were like a fairground and most people thought that they had had a good night out for very little expense.

"The children got a good supply of sweets as well, for there were several cut-price sweet shops adjoining the markets. One of the sights was the group of nuns who used to come to the market and stand silently holding out buckets which were always filled with fresh fish for the children they cared for. Only when the bucket was filled would they speak, and then they would say 'God be with you' and go away until the next Saturday night."

When Mr. and Mrs. Brokenbrow retired in 1973, the business was handed on to their nephew and son-in-law.

Up to the coming of the railways and the building of the suburbs, a remarkable amount of the fruit and vegetables in the Bristol markets was grown in and around the city. One reminder that Bristol once had a patchwork of orchards and market gardens is the

Rhubarb Tavern at Barton Hill, which stands on the edge of the site where there were rhubarb fields.

Medieval Bristol was surrounded by farms, market gardens and orchards; the monks at Greyfriars and Whitefriars, now huge office blocks, grew produce there to support their monasteries. The earliest mention of a professional market gardener in the city, according to market garden historian Gilbert Roberts, is of Joseph Elton – one of the Clevedon family – who was gardening in 1650. He was also a scavenger, collecting night soil to fertilise his land, something all subsequent market gardeners did.

By the beginning of the 19th century, there were dozens of market gardeners working quite near the city, in Barton Hill, Easton, Lawrence Hill, Whitehall and St. George, but as the houses and the railway lines encroached, they were pushed further out to the edges of the city. Often they built on their land grand houses which still stand among the Victorian villas.

All traces of these gardening families, the Gerrishes, the Fords, the Hemmings and the Thatchers, who all inter-married and formed a huge tribe in the city, have vanished, except for the Roberts family, who now have market gardens at Frenchay and Stapleton. **Roberts Bros.** was founded by a butcher, George Tyler, in 1829, when he bought three cottages and an acre or so of land at Croft End, St. George. He grew all the usual crops, plus celery and rhubarb, for the Bristol Market, and took on colliers from the near-by pit as casual labour at busy times. His grand-daughter Martha carried on the business when he died – market gardeners were quite often women – and she married George Roberts, a baker, in 1877: her grandsons and great-grandsons run the business now.

Martha was a formidable woman who, to make ends meet, took a "board" at the Market, and went around the cottage gardens buying herbs and flowers which she bunched to sell at St. Nicholas, in two baskets. She also bought and sold in the market, and had to borrow 30 shillings to cover her first day's trading; she used to take her children with her to work. When her father died, the market garden was put up for auction, and she bought it on a mortgage. It took her until 1916 to pay it off, and she travelled all over the area buying and selling produce, while her family ran the small-holding. The Croft End land was compulsorily purchased by Bristol Corporation in 1936, but they allowed Martha to stay in the house which her grandfather had built, until she died in 1948. By then her home was in the middle of a sea of prefabs.

With the money from the sale of the land, her two grandsons Fred and Gilbert bought a small holding at Stapleton, and vegetables are still grown there to this day.

Another connection with the market garden world is the firm of **Crispins,** of Cheltenham Road. Nowadays they deal in heating and ventilation equipment, but in the last century they built greenhouses. James Crispin founded the business and in 1821 indentured his son, John Farmer Crispin, as a carpenter. They saw that the rich middle class Bristolians in their big houses would want conservatories and greenhouses, and started to design and make them. James was a Fellow of the Royal Horticultural Society, so he knew what gardening requirements were.

From building greenhouses it was an easy step to heating them, and the firm began to style themselves horticultural builders and heating engineers. They started trading in

Nelson Street, but in the 1880s moved to a large site in Silverthorne Lane, and were such successful specialists that they won medals for their heating installations at the Liverpool Show of 1886. John Crispin's sons George and Henry branched out into making heating boilers for commercial and industrial use; the giant Victorian boilers that they installed can still be seen in some Bristol churches, and to this day, the firm services boilers in several famous independent schools in the city. Greenhouses were made until the 1930s, but the compulsory purchase of all their timber in the First World War hit the business and in any case the demand for greenhouses declined – so they switched over to heating and ventilating instead.

Though the Bristol fruit and vegetable markets were still important, by the Victorian period greengrocers' shops had become more common, especially in the suburbs. One of them was started by **Emily Smele** in 1882 in Mill Lane, Bedminster, and she did so well that branches were opened in Raleigh Road, Midland Road and Castle Street. Emily was the first greengrocer in Bristol to sell bananas, which first came to the city in 1901. Her son George took over and opened further branches in Stapleton Road, Downend and Winterbourne; his son Jim, the present owner, who has just retired and passed the business on to his daughter, spent his babyhood in a pram in the shop. He took over in 1946, and can remember as a schoolboy how boats would bring imported potatoes right up to Bristol Bridge, where he would buy five tons, which would be sold in the shop between mid-day and midnight. "Now we don't sell five tons in a fortnight," he says. "Another speciality was soaked peas. We used to put two hundredweight to soak and sell them for tuppence a pint. If someone bought ten pints, they got one free. Some of the produce was still grown locally when I was a boy: we used to cut savoys out at Cleeve. And the displays in the greengrocery shops before the last war were beautiful: we used to spend all day Monday doing them – a real work of art they were." Of all the Smele branches, only one now remains, at Winterbourne.

Of the hundreds and hundreds of Victorian bakers, only one has survived over a century: **John Williams** of Cheltenham Road. The firm was started by his grandfather Charles Henry Williams who, after serving an apprenticeship in Tetbury, moved to Yatton Keynall, on the Bristol-Chippenham road, to the Eight Bells public house, where in 1884 he was employed as a brewer and baker. The connection was yeast: commercial yeast was not used by bakers until the turn of the century; instead they used brewers' yeast raised from barley, or potato barm, making Victorian bread that was much stronger-tasting than ours.

Charles Henry's wife Dorcas Charlotte was the schoolmistress daughter of a local farmer who was also a carrier; he used to drive into Bristol selling his produce as he went, and buying items to sell on the way home. He used to cry his wares as he came to each village, hence his ironic nickname Whispering Jim. Through him, his son-in-law found a job in Old Market in 1888, working at the Old Custom House, No.78, where in return for caretaking he was allowed to make and sell bread. He and his wife lived in a cottage at the back. From there he moved to his own bakery at 12 Penn Street (now the site of C and A's) in 1912, and one of his five sons, Albert, joined the business.

At first he traded with a handcart and a bicycle, walking as far as Troopers Hill in Kingswood to raise enough in sales to buy the next batch of flour – which he could buy in

Broadmead from Henry Jones, the Bristol inventor of self-raising flour. His son, John Williams, can remember sleeping on pillow-cases made from flour-sacks. He went to school in the nearby Quakers Friars, where the old Bakers' Hall was situated.

The firm stayed in Penn Street until 1939, when there was a slum clearance scheme, with compulsory purchase, and Albert took over an existing bakery at Cheltenham Road. The Penn Street premises remained empty, and were still standing in the Fifties, one of the few that Hitler missed. John Williams took over in 1954, and has since opened seven branches. He says the trade is just as hard as it was in his grandfather's day, with a 2 a.m. baking and dawn deliveries. The great difference is in the number of non-bread items – 150 of them – that he makes; in Victorian times, bakers and confectioners were quite separate. And the number of local bakers has decreased dramatically: between the wars there were over 400 members of the Bristol Master Bakers' Federation. Now there are 43.

One of the old ovens still in John Williams' bakery was made in the last century by the firm of **Thomas Collins,** who now trade at Kingswood. They were founded in 1877 as suppliers to the bakery trade, and his steam tube ovens were made to last: several are still functioning. This type of oven was standard right up to the 1950s, when the plant bakers arrived with their steamed sliced bread, driving many small bakers out of business. The change hit Thomas Collins initially, but they adapted and have benefited greatly from the reaction against mass-produced factory breads, and the return of the small baker to "real" bread.

Collins were famous in the trade for their twin deck ovens, which worked at independent temperatures, so that a baker could cook bread in one and dough-based cakes in the other. The *Baker* magazine in 1893 described one oven as being able to cope with 200 sacks of flour made up, per week, using two tons of coke. Collins held a competition for Bristol bakers who had his ovens, and as a result of the publicity received orders from as far away as London.

Another firm supplying bakers originally was **Lentons,** of Jacob Street. John Lenton came to Bristol in 1881 to set up in Rosemary Street as an ironmonger, plumber and sheet metal worker. He soon moved to Merchant Street and was joined by his three sons; they started specialising in making tins for the bakery trade and paint firms, and made funnels and measures. After the First World War they moved to their present home and the third generation of the family took over in the 1950s. They now trade solely as sheet metal workers specialising in machine guards, ductwork for air conditioning and specialist one-off items.

Of all the food trades, butchery was the earliest to take to specialist shops; William of Wycestre mentions the butchers' shops at Temple Gate in 15th century Bristol. Like every other trade, it was governed by its guild, the Butchers' Company, and the Corporation, with rules about which day slaughtering could be done, selling in Lent, where meat could be sold – which was in certain streets until the end of the 16th century, when a meat market was established. A regulation number of "foreign" sellers of meat and poultry were allowed, much to the Bristol butchers' disgust. A non-butcher who slaughtered an animal could be fined, and even the way the meat was presented was under control.

In 1736 a butcher was convicted for "exposing for sale in Broad Street an old ewe, dressed up in the same manner as lamb", and fined 40s. The street sellers in Broad Street and High Street became such a nuisance that in 1735, plans were started to build a new market, the Exchange and St. Nicholas Market, in Corn Street, and the butchers moved there.

But some butchers sold from shops in the suburbs, and two of the 18th century firms, amazingly, are still trading.

The earlier is **Collards,** of North Street, Bedminster. The family legend is that in 1770, Edward Collard came on a visit to Bristol from his home at Enmore, near Bridgwater, in a horse-and-cart. The horse went lame, so Edward stayed overnight with his Bristol uncle, and decided there and then to open a butcher's shop in Temple Street.

By the 1850s, his son Aldred was also trading at 7, Whitehouse Street, Bedminster, where he had a slaughterhouse, and by the 1880s, there was son Clifford with a shop in Old Market, and son Charles Edward at Redcliff Hill and another shop in Victoria Street. There was a branch, too, at Clifton for a while, but this was given up – apparently Cliftonians were not prompt enough about paying their bills.

Aldred Collard was also something of a poet: he wrote dozens of long poems about the local scene, the trams, the Downs, the Suspension Bridge, and the Bristol Steam Roller, and he had a head of Poet Laureate Robert Southey sculpted to put over a North Street doorway, on the corner of Merrywood Road, presumed the site of Southey's grandfather's Georgian home. Here is a sample of Aldred's verse:

"Who is there alive who has not been to town,
Or walked along streets where the rails are laid down,
But has seen the tram-cars, so lofty and bright-
Fitted with splendour and illuminated at night-
Also noticed the horses, so used to the track,
And don't know the sound of their clickety clack?"

His son, another Aldred, married Florence Louisa Melinda, daughter of another butcher, Mr. Woodall (the wedding reception was held in the freshly whitewashed slaughterhouse in Whitehouse Street) and it was this couple who opened the present shop in North Street. Florence Collard got fed up, in 1899, with living with her in-laws, and one day out pushing the pram, she noticed the shop was for sale, persuaded her husband to buy it and they moved in the next day. She was a great force in the business, coping single-handed in the First World War: she once drove a horse-and-cart to Victoria Street and dumped a rotten side of beef outside the Ministry of Agriculture offices. She worked in the shop until she was in her eighties, and died in 1968.

Almost as old is the firm of **T.J. Wise,** which now has the seventh generation of the family in charge at Whiteladies Road. James Wise started his business in 1793, at Temple Gate, in a house almost opposite what is now the station incline. He came from a large family who worked mainly as carpenters and wheelwrights and undertakers, and the family can be traced back to Keynsham in the early 1700s. The carpentering side of the family business ended in the 1850s.

James Wise had a slaughterhouse at the back of his property and was registered in the city as "slaughterer no.1." The family owned several shops in Bath Parade and by 1854

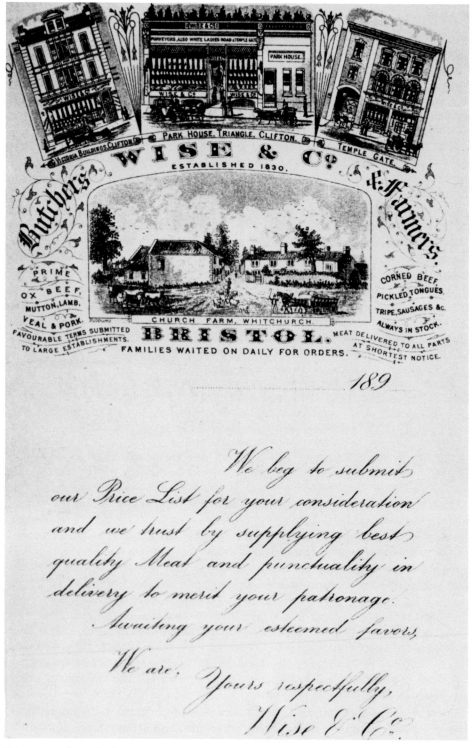

This masterpiece of advertising engraving shows Wise & Co's three shops, their Whitchurch farm, and the respectful message to prospective customers of the 1890s.

James' son George had a butcher's shop there, next door to his carpenter cousin, Thomas. The firm obviously flourished, because in the second half of the 19th century there were branches at Triangle Place, Whiteladies Road and Avonmouth, and a farm was bought at Whitchurch, on the site of what was to be Bristol's first aerodrome.

A succession of Jameses and Thomases and Thomas Jameses ran the business, which was big enough to keep a fleet of horses and carts for deliveries, and the family lived in Whiteladies Road in the grand houses now occupied by the BBC. The grandfather of the present owner, Allen Wise, was a Bristol character: he was Lord Mayor, and his hobby was water-divining – he discovered a well at Ham Green Hospital. One of his employees, taken on in 1893, as a cycle boy, was Ernest Bevin.

Before the Second World War, the Whiteladies Road branch was the busiest butcher's shop in Bristol, needing six boys and three vans to make deliveries of orders which were taken on the phone by three girls. The farm was kept on until 1936, when the stock, which included sheep, cattle, hens, horses and pigs, was auctioned off for only £1,053 4s. 10d.

During the Second World War, Wise's was one of the two Bristol slaughterers given Ministry contracts, and the firm's cold stores at Avonmouth had a strange cargo in 1944: they housed and hid ships taking part in the D-Day operation. After the war a new venture was three Sam Small shops, but gradually the business contracted, so that nowadays it trades as a contract butchery only. And sadly, there is no James or Thomas of the eighth generation to take on the family tradition.

Moving to drink, one is not surprised to find that several wine firms have survived for two centuries or more; Bristol was famous as a wine port from the 12th century onwards, and the first recorded import of wine is in 1180. French wine began flowing into Bristol after Henry II married Eleanor of Aquitaine, German wine arrived in the 14th century, followed by wine from all round the Mediterranean from the 15th century on; it was a staple drink, along with beer, when pure drinking water was in short supply. Sherry, the wine most identified with Bristol, is first mentioned as an import in the mid-17th century.

The oldest surviving wine firm is **J.R. Phillips,** founded in 1739 by William George, whose sons Philip and James both had a great effect on Bristol's drinking habits. William set up as a wine merchant and distiller at 59, Baldwin Street, and the two sons carried on the business until 1781, when Philip left to start a brewery in Counterslip, George's Brewery. James transferred the wine business to Queen Charlotte Street, trading as a hop and brandy merchant, and in 1804 bought a house, warehouse and cellar at 6, King Street, for £1,366 15s. 11d. (It still stands, on the corner next to the Llandoger Trow). The firm's earliest ledger in existence shows the extensive trade in foreign wines and spirits which James George carried on. An entry for 1791 shows a then considerable sum, £219, paid to the Collector of Customs; in 1806 the firm imported 5,694 gallons of brandy.

By the turn of the century an accountant named James Rouquet Phillips was employed: his ledger shows that one of their customers was Perry and Urch, the firm which was to become Harveys. The Napoleonic Wars, which cut down greatly the amount of wine and spirits imported into Bristol, does not seem to have affected the

Harvey's wines and sherries came right into the heart of the city: unloading on the docks, 1930s.

From ship to shore. Avery's men rolled out the barrels from the docks to their cellars in Frog Lane and Denmark Street.

business; in 1808 a stocktaking revealed that they had 4,578 gallons of Cognac brandy at 21s. a gallon, worth £4,804 at a time of sea blockades. This was the year that James Phillips was made a partner, and in 1810 they moved to Nelson Street where they traded for the next 150 years.

James George became a substantial citizen, and was invited to become senior partner in the Castle Bank at the Old Dutch House. After his father's death, James George junior sold out to James Phillips in 1825. At this point, the firm, like many other wine firms in the city, was in decline because of heavy duties on French imports; consumption fell and tea became a serious rival. Things improved in 1831 when import dues were eased, and Phillips built up a network of customers all over the country and abroad in Holland, Germany and the West Indies. James's two sons, William and Augustus, took over in 1836 but couldn't agree, so they came to the strange arrangement that each should run the firm for alternate fortnights! It seemed to work, for profits went up. William retired in 1879, taking with him £10,000 in cash and £16,671 in shares, while Augustus stayed on, ruling like a despot. In 1889, he converted the firm into one of the first private limited companies in Bristol, with himself as Governing Director, giving him total power. He died in 1896, just two years before the firm adopted that wild new idea, electric light. It was about this time that they gave up their interest in three trading ships.

Into this century, Phillips continued to sell another 18th century line, old English cordials such as shrub and lime juice, which went on all the ships from Bristol as a means of preventing scurvy. Their sale of port also dated from 1789. After the last war, they moved the entire operation, which is now a wholesale agency, to Avonmouth, leaving empty the vast cellars on two levels under the Colston Hall, and the only vestige left of the Great House, built there in the 16th century.

J.R. Phillips is now owned by Allied Lyons and Whitbreads.

Next oldest, chronologically, is **Avery's,** established in 1793 in premises which had been used for the storage if not for the sale of alcohol since early in the century. The building (still Avery's cellars) stood on the cross-roads of Frog Lane and what was to be Park Street, conveniently near the docks.

But the Avery family did not enter the picture until 1851 when John Avery took the premises over after a bankruptcy. (During the bankruptcy proceedings, ironically, the firm had briefly been in the possession of the Harvey family).

Under a street improvement programme started in 1865, part of the frontage of the Avery premises was sold. The remainder was rebuilt and extended to a frontage on the by then fashionable Park Street. In 1878, John Avery's three sons took over, and from a modest £6,000 in 1880, sales grew to £9,000 in 1891; 1897 was an incredible boom year with nine and a half million bottles of champagne sold nationally – it was Queen Victoria's Diamond Jubilee Year. In the Nineties, Avery's sold not only to much of middle class Bristol but also to customers in the Midlands, South Wales and Cornwall. Sales were mainly of sherry, port, burgundy, claret and champagne.

Shorter opening hours and stiff drink regulations from the teetotal Lloyd George in the First World War hit Avery's as it did every wine firm, and sales dipped as wine prices rose, but once the war ended, consumption soared again. The man who was to make Avery's famous in this century, Ronald Avery, made an inauspicious start: he was teetotal until the age of 20. But his arrival at the firm in 1923 marked a development of the fine wine side of the business, with less emphasis on bar sales. He started to build up direct contacts with the vineyards, instead of using an agent, and his legendary tasting skill and nose for quality became the cornerstone of the business.

It was he who rebuilt in 1936 the bars that were next door to the shop, using fittings from the famous ship, the Mauretania, and he also installed a revolutionary new bottle-washing system in the warehouse: each bottle was filled about a third full with lead shot and vinegar, agitated and then rinsed out with hot and cold water. After two or three washings, the shot pocked the inside of the bottle, offering an advantage to wines to be laid down for a long period, for the marks collected the sediment. When the Second World War came, the precious fine wines were evacuated out of the city by pony and trap for safe-keeping at Frampton Cotterell, and the wine and food business at the Mauretania virtually hibernated. After the war, and Ronald Avery's death, his son John took over, the fourth generation of fine noses.

When mothers wanted to frighten their children in 18th century Bristol, they threatened them with a visit from the ruthless sea-captain Thomas Harvey who sailed the routes to Spain, Portugal and the West Indies. His son was a seaman, too, but he married a Bristol girl, Anne Urch, in 1805, and settled down. He had a son, John, who forsook the high seas for the wine trade, and this is how **Harvey's** began. His uncle Thomas Urch was in the wine trade, working for William Perry who kept cellars in Denmark Street, and in 1822 young John joined him to learn the business. By 1840 he was a partner and eventually he took control. Since all the family records were destroyed in the 1940 Blitz, little is known about him except that he was a collector of fine glass, that he played the flute, and fathered eight children. His sons John and Edward both went into the wine trade and in 1871 the firm became known as John Harvey and Sons.

Both sons were keen travellers and went to the wine producers to taste before buying. It was John Harvey II who made all the business contacts, getting orders from gentlemen's clubs and regimental messes, and he founded Harvey's export trade: the first order went to Mombasa in 1884. Edward was the administrator, though he could spring surprises: he married unexpectedly, at the age of 50, and his staff toasted him in Perrier-Jouet '74. The firm at this time was naturally selling sherry and port, Bordeaux, Burgundy and Rhine wines, and in 1882 they hit on a best-seller, Bristol Cream. In 1886 they started supplying the Royal Household; Queen Victoria, or rather the Master of the Royal Cellars, ordered 115 cases of the '91 Medoc.

John Harvey III became chairman in 1910, when port was the top seller, doctors having pronounced that sherry was bad for the liver. During the First World War, staff at Harveys worked overtime to supply naval and military messes in the battle-zones and military hospitals – at that time the standard prescription for treating heavy blood loss was Burgundy or claret. Cases stencilled with the name of Harveys became a regular feature of battlefield debris, and a bottle of Harvey's Hunting Port, later returned to the firm by Admiral Beatty, was the only breakable object in the wardroom of the flagship *Lion* to survive the bombardment at the battle of Jutland.

Eddy Harvey succeeded in 1919 to a world of change, when a new kind of customer, the man in the street, began to emerge, and the firm for the first time advertised in a big way. Machinery began to arrive at the bottling plant, and there was a welcome boost in their export trade when America was freed from Prohibition.

In 1938, Eddy Harvey handed over to "Mr. Jack," John Harvey IV, only to see, two years later, Harvey's in Denmark Street a war-blasted ruin. Mercifully the medieval cellars under the building survived intact, and since the war prevented exports, sufficient stocks were left to continue trading. By 1954 a new office was built, and by 1959, sales stood at £4 million. In 1958 they raised the money to build their new plant at Whitchurch, with George McWatters, grandson of Edward Harvey, as chairman, and they found new partners in Cockburn Smithies, the port firm. In 1966 they became part of Showerings which in 1968 merged with Allied Breweries, but there is still a John Harvey, the fifth, at the helm. The palate as well as the name truly seem to be inherited.

Not much is known about **Howells** of Small Street, but they certainly have the oldest cellars in the city. Under their home, the house built by wealthy merchant John Foster in 1481, are extensive vaults which have been used for storing wine ever since. Edward Slingsby Howell started his business in the early 19th century, and it then passed to various other people until his great grandson Colonel John Mallard eventually inherited. He sold out in 1957 and there the family connection died. Few records remain except for ledgers for 1909 which show that a hogshead of brandy – 24 dozen bottles – sold for a mere £85.

Other firms started up to serve the wine trade. In 1834 the Edwards family of Devon, ship-builders and merchants, sent their son John in his schooner *The Lady of the Lake* on a wine-buying trip; from Charentes in France he brought a cargo back to Gloucester and Bristol and among his customers were Avery's and Harvey's. It was the beginning of a wine shipping business and Avery's showed enough confidence in the young master mariner to buy shares in the new ships he was commissioning. John Edwards set up a counting house on the Quay in 1846 and became established in the city as a ship-owner and shipbroker. He took his son-in-law William Turner on in 1850, giving the firm its present title of **Turner Edwards.**

Wine shipping was a risky business. John Edwards had to find the money to build his ship, fit it out, pay the crew and be responsible to the growers and wine merchants for cargoes worth many thousands of pounds. All could be lost through bad weather or faulty navigation. A charter signed in 1843 seems to imply that Edwards received £225 for every one hundred "tuns" of wine safely delivered, and he also sold an outward cargo, usually coal, to a port in S.W. France or Portugal.

As managing owner he had to be skilled in several trades, including accounting, and had to have a knowledge of French. Between 1845 and his death in 1860, he commissioned fifteen schooners, wood built, 70-80 feet long, and loaded up to 200 tons; the sails were mainly of the fore and aft variety and could be handled by six men and a boy. In all his years as a mariner and ship-owner, he only ever lost three vessels.

William Turner bought shares not just in the wine ships but in ocean going barques, which he used to develop a trade with South America in skins and fertiliser; he also had interests in coastal-going schooners which sold parcels of wine at ports on the south and west coasts, and bought shares in the early steam propelled ships, which he later used for the wine trade. The years 1850-1900 were Turner Edwards' heyday as a ship-owning company; during those years they were majority share-holders in a fleet of 34 ships.

After Turner's death, the company under John Edwards II opened runs up to Cadiz, and round Cape Horn, but world demand for ships, after the boom of the Crimean War and the American Civil War, came to an end and the fleet was cut down to one wine ship in the 1890s. A relative by marriage, John Fowler, and a young accountant, Herbert Nethercott, took over and bought cheaply in 1901 a steamship which was used first to load coal at Swansea or tinplate from South Wales, for delivery in Europe; she would call at a number of wine ports after the cargo was sold, and then return to Bristol. But the First World War brought another slump: their steamship, the *Sir Walter,* was torpedoed on government service, and for the first time in their history the company had no ship at sea. Then came the Depression, and in 1934 the company's last ship was sold, exactly 100 years after the business had started.

Reorganisation allowed a new company to be set up; two new ships were chartered and started runs which covered six wine ports in Europe, a venture brought to an abrupt halt by the next war. They started up again afterwards, but the decline of Bristol as a wine port went on, and the last sea-hauled wine cargo came in 1971. For a few years, bottling was carried out, but the new direction was to handle wine packed in cartons, not casks, using road and rail links. Today the company's main function is as a freight distributor rather than as a shipper, with facilities in one of Bristol's famous redbrick bonded warehouses.

An industry which grew up to serve the drinks trade was bottle and cask dealing. In 1850, at a time when glass was still being manufactured at two kilns in the city, William Henry Isaac **Rawlings,** who had been running a popular coffee house in Denmark Street, changed trades to become a bottle dealer, setting up at 1, Marsh Street.

Nowadays bottles are rarely re-used, but in Victorian Bristol, bottle dealers travelled far and wide buying up used bottles, which they would clean, and then sell to the local wine and spirit firms. William Rawlings also bought the casks in which the wine and spirit arrived at the port, and resold them, mainly to cider makers and whisky distillers, who particularly prized the sherry casks because they imparted a special flavour to the Scotch. He stored the casks in railway arches under Temple Meads and in cellars under the Hippodrome, and used to travel with a horse and dray to Taunton market every week, to sell casks to the cider makers.

Rawlings became an international dealer in glass when he secured an agreement with a German bottle manufacturer, and became the principal importer in Britain, a deal which brought him great prosperity, until the Free Trade policy ended with the First World War, and he had to buy English glass. By then he could not buy it in Bristol – the last kiln closed in 1923.

William Rawlings died in 1927, and his son William Henry took over. He only lived another ten years, and in 1937, Leonard Routley, who had joined the firm as a 15 year-old schoolboy in 1927, formed a limited company, and took over with the help of two sleeping partners. When they died, Leonard Routley bought up their shares, and became sole owner.

He can remember the days when the firm owned a big dray-horse called Prince: "One year, at the Remembrance Day Parade in the Centre, he caused chaos by bolting when the maroons went off. I used to drive him twice a week to Bath, delivering bottles." Another line Mr. Routley remembers was straw collars, made by the million to protect bottles from breakages.

The Marsh Street premises were bombed in 1940, and the firm moved to Brunswick Street. Since there was in war-time a severe shortage of glass, Rawlings' plant became the central depot in England for collecting and re-distributing the Ministry of Food welfare orange bottles which were issued to mothers at clinics. Leonard Routley and his wife Nora worked round the clock sterilising millions of these 6oz. bottles, packing them, and sending them back to the bottlers.

After the war, when the re-use of bottles became less common, the firm became importers of glass from makers all over the world, and now are the largest independent glass suppliers to such companies as Boots, Robertson's Jams and the Taunton Cider Company, as well as local wine firms. The cask side of the business died out when wine and spirits began to arrive in containers, or already bottled.

Leonard Routley's son John is now the Managing Director, and the firm's headquarters is currently at Cecil Road, Kingswood.

The supply of drinking water in Bristol, up to the mid-19th century, was erratic, and unsafe, so it was a case of "let them drink beer." Latimer says that in 1700, the price of strong beer was only sixpence a gallon, and that Bristolians drank it for breakfast, lunch and dinner. Beer brewed for home consumption cost only 2d. a gallon.

At that time Bristol had 240 inns, taverns and alehouses, one for every 20 families in the city – and the penalty for drunkenness was six hours in the stocks.

Dozens of small breweries flourished at this period, and in 1702, one of them, by Bristol Bridge, was owned by the Mayor, Sir John Hawkins; this business was the ancestor of The Bristol Brewery, which produced **George's** and now **Courage's** beer.

In 1730 the brewery was bought by wealthy slave merchant Isaac Hobhouse and his sons John and Henry built the Porter Brewery that is the basis of the modern complex. This business passed in 1788 to Philip George, who with six other Bristol merchants, bought a malthouse in Tucker Street and set up as The Philip George Bristol Brewery.

An advertisement in *Felix Farley's Journal,* 1794, says: "P. George, Bristol Porter and Beer Company will deliver in barrels and half barrels their Porter to all towns and villages within five miles of the City and is sold at Fourpence per Quart."

Brewing was a cut-throat business so George sent a traveller to Ireland to sell the porter – and sold 60,000 barrels a year there. By the beginning of the 19th century George's brewery was acquiring other small brewery businesses and a brewery war began: it was of course won by George's, who in 1878 bought 70 licenced houses as well. That year they went public and within five years their shares had brought in nearly six and a half million pounds, enough to wipe out many of their small competitors.

By the turn of this century there was only one big local rival left, Bristol United Breweries, which merged with George's in 1952. In 1961, the firm amalgamated with Courage's, who in 1972 were taken over by Imperial. They in turn were taken over by the Hanson Trust, who sold Courage's in 1986 to the Elders IXL group.

Bristol's first motor bus service ran direct to John Cordeux's store in Merchant Road, Clifton, seen here in 1906.

Keeping skirt and blouse together was a problem, hence this patent device, advertised in Baker Baker's wholesale catalogue for Spring and Summer, 1912.

4 – "O Lord, send them in, send them in"

John Cordeux
Clifton department store owner

Shopping for clothes in Bristol, until quite late in the 19th century, meant shopping for material: either the shop provided a dressmaking service or you went to your private dressmaker.

Only children's wear, some underwear, and cloaks or mantles were bought ready-made. The rest – coats, dresses, men's suits and shirts, servants' wear, mourning, and so on – all had to be made up, and the prejudice against ready-made clothes, which were thought very working-class, continued into the 1920s and 30s.

But Bristol, being a port, did have a ready-to-wear trade. In fact a long-gone tailoring firm, Cole and Pottow, who traded in Maudlin Street and Avonmouth, are credited with inventing the man's ready-to-wear three-piece suit. Sailors and travellers who arrived at the port would buy ready-made shirts and cheap suits, and the fact that we have a surviving wholesale clothes manufacturer, **Wathen Gardiner,** is due to the port: this firm was able to export vast quantities of clothes to the colonies and elsewhere.

Wathen Gardiner started something entirely new when clothier John Gardiner, High Sheriff of Bristol in 1810, had his brain-wave. With remarkable foresight, this Bridge Street trader realised that there was a profitable market for ready-made clothes in the West Indies. His shirts and suits were packed into puncheons aboard ships bound for the West Indies, and the puncheons came back filled with rum.

John Gardiner, who was Postmaster of Bristol from 1825 to 1832, and had to save the mail during the Bristol Riots, founded another empire indirectly: his son Alfred became the founder of Gardiner's the iron merchants. His other son John took over the clothing business in the 1840s, expanding to build factories in Broad Street, Tower Lane, John Street and Little John Street.

In 1854, the firm started trading with Australasia and a measure of how respected the business was is the fact that Mr., later Sir Charles Wathen, a prominent local citizen who was Lord Mayor six times, joined as a partner in 1862.

The export trade was so huge that in 1899 the firm had to re-locate in a new purpose-built factory at Staple Hill, its present home. On the two-acre site the factory was built using the new principle of northern light, for the 400 staff (hundreds more worked as outworkers) in the cutting room, the making-up department and other rooms where trimming, packing, measuring and fitting were done, needed maximum daylight. An unusual feature was the practice of fitting every garment on a real man or boy of the right size, instead of on a dummy. The brand-name for the clothes in 1910 was "Xtra-good"; this was the year of their centenary, when they set up training schemes in factories in Frampton Cotterell, Winterbourne and Mangotsfield. The firm had a London office, and representatives toured all over Britain and the colonies.

Today, although trade with the former colonies has diminished, Wathen Gardiner have opened another factory at Calne, to help supply the British fashion market, and their latest venture is a youth training scheme.

The poor of Bristol, up to this century, shopped for clothes in markets, and bought from stalls and barrows and second-hand clothes shops; in the Victorian period they would certainly have not dared to venture into Bristol's posh drapery shops.

Drapery is one of the city's oldest trades, started in the days when Bristol had a wool trade, and selling wool, linen and cotton fabrics, haberdashery and hosiery.

Most drapers were in the High Street and Wine Street areas, the most sought-after sites up to the Blitz. (Not one of these general drapers' stores has survived: the last examples, Miles of Bedminster and Prossers and Connett's of Clifton closed quite recently.)

By the early 19th century, draperies had become shops on the modern pattern, buying in goods from London or abroad, rather than from local weavers. We know exactly what a Wine Street draper's business was like in Regency times, because a London draper, William Ablett, came to manage a shop there around 1820, and wrote about it in his *Reminiscences of an Old Draper*. He tells how old-fashioned the Bristol traders were: "Trade was conducted in a droning sort of way", and how he shocked them by his new fangled ideas about window-dressing several times a week, with lavish displays of shawls and bolts of fabric, and selling special lines to pedlars. The general view was that a draper should stick to what he had learned as an apprentice, and not go in for flashy salesmanship, as Ablett did, selling umbrellas outside the shop when it rained. Draper Thomas Jones, who set up his department store in Wine Street in 1843, was considered outrageous for selling not just drapery items, but anything on which he could make a profit.

In the roll-call of Bristol's long-established department stores, there has to be some cheating. Though some of them survive, their names, or their function have changed. Jolly's still trade, but only in Bath; Alexandra have given up their store and turned to workwear, Jones has become Debenhams, and Baker Baker, once retailers as well as wholesalers, now trade only as wholesalers.

In the Victorian heyday, Bristol had six department stores: Jones, Baker Baker, Alexandra, Jolly, J.F. Taylor, and **Cordeux's** of Clifton. The last named was started by a family of drapers in St. James Barton; in the 1860s they moved to Merchants Road and Regent Street, where they grew into a store which stretched from where Hartwell's is now, right round to Saville Place, with a huge workroom, a warehouse, accommodation for staff above, and a name for selling exotic imported goods. A commentator in the 1890s said the shop was "like a visit to the gorgeous bazaars of the Orient." Cordeux's (which Bristolians called Cordews) had 45 departments and employed 300 assistants, and arranged with Bristol Tramways Company to have the trams stop outside. They seem to have closed down around the First World War, after moving to Queen's Road in 1909.

The department store is always held to be a French idea which was copied in London, but in fact there were department stores of a sort in the provinces long before the London ones, with different sorts of goods in separate rooms, and a new policy, offering no abatement on prices – up to this stage, customers usually had to haggle.

James Jolly opened his shop in Milsom Street, Bath, in 1830, announcing that it was an Emporium combining a shop and a bazaar, where he would accept only ready money. Besides drapery and haberdashery, he sold foreign china and knick-knacks, hosiery, lace nets, ormulu clocks, British and foreign cabinet goods, jewellery, perfume, stationery, brushes, cutlery and toys. He gradually took over the adjoining houses and did so well that a Bristol branch was opened in 1858 at College Green. With James Jolly's son William as manager, they specialised in fine silks and cashmeres, and at one stage described themselves as silk mercers to Queen Mary; they also provided a baby-linen room and a café. But the Bristol store was never as successful as the Bath one, and in 1888 it was sold off. A later generation of the Jolly family bought in back in 1923, and when the store was bombed in 1940, they moved to two shops in Whiteladies Road, where they remained until 1977, until the House of Fraser, the new owners, closed it down.

Unlike the Jolly's, **Thomas Jones,** the Pembrokeshire draper who came to Wine Street in 1843, was not after the genteel trade. He was after sheer profit and to this end sold anything: cheese, tobacco, beer, all went in the window along with silks and satins, and all his competitors thought he was outrageous. Not for nothing did he display the slogan "Right Against Might."

He was an early exploiter of publicity, too: he would be the talk of Bristol for his wild window-displays, clearing the window of drapery to display two live Welsh ponies, or a show of cheeses. After the Crimean War ended in 1856, he bought up military uniforms for his assistants and Army harness for his delivery horses, and got his assistants to ride the horses in parade through the streets, thus ensuring that everyone would talk about his store.

By 1865 he had moved into Nos 56–63 Wine Street and was described as "a whole sale and retail silk mercers, drapers and haberdashers, agents for Tetley and Sons, pale ale brewers and dealer in Cumberland hams."

Thomas Jones's success meant that he constantly had to expand the business, and so did his successors; by 1939 there were ten Wine Street shops, three in the High Street and three in Mary-le-Port. The firm tried to buy the old Dutch House in the Twenties, and when they failed, embarked on a huge modernisation programme, installing lifts for the first time. The work was almost finished when in 1940 the whole street was flattened by bombs. The response of the staff was to carry on the firm's restaurant service on the street, using salvaged rafters as fuel. The store moved up to Beacon House in Queen's Road, and took on other shops in Clifton, Wells Road, Broadmead, Merchant Street, Staple Hill and Kingswood. When the new Broadmead shopping centre was being planned, Jones was the first major store to take a site. They opened in 1957, and were eventually taken over by Debenhams in 1972.

The use of the word "warehouse" in the past was ambiguous. Originally, a warehouse was literally a place where wares were stored; but in the early 19th century it could also be a grand name for a retail shop that was larger than usual. It also became the practice for drapers to have two sets of prices, one for wholesale and one for retail sales, and this became confusing, so the wholesale side was hived off into a warehouse.

This is presumably what happened with **Baker Baker,** who were founded in the 1840s. William Mills Baker and Thomas Baker came to Bristol to seek their fortunes in the drapery trade and joined the Wine Street firm of Culverwell and Co. By 1857 William had worked hard enough to buy into a partnership, and Thomas followed suit in 1860.

By 1883, the Baker family was in control.

There were two distinct operations: wholesaling to the drapery and department store trade, and retailing. By the Thirties, Baker Baker had three huge stores in Bridge Street, Wine Street and Mary-le-Port. One set of buildings was entirely for wholesale goods, while Bridge Street was entirely retail.

The entire empire was razed to the ground in the Blitz; in vain had the Air Raid Precautions booklet told the staff to "courteously invite the Customer to go down to the Shelter with the Assistant, or immediately leave." It was fortunate that the bombs fell at night.

The business was then crammed into eight houses in Queen Charlotte Street, buildings which had been used to accommodate women staff, and by 1959 a new warehouse had been built in Thomas Street and a retail store opened in College Green (though this became McIlroys in 1969). The fourth generation of the Baker family is still in charge; the firm was taken over by Courtaulds in 1963 but in 1982 reverted back to being a private company, and the retailing side ended; the headquarters and warehouse are now at Feeder Road.

A glimpse of wholesaling just before the First World War is possible because the Baker Baker Spring Catalogue of 1912 has survived. 640 pages long, it was sent out to retail drapers and haberdashers. Private customers were plainly a problem, because the preface says that the firm has received complaints from wholesale customers that "people not in the trade" have been buying through introductions, and appeals for an end to "this unsatisfactory practice."

The catalogue lists departments ranging from grey calicos to china, cocoa mats, belts and trimmings, corsets and baby linens, tapestries and floorcloths, waterproof cloaks and electro-plated cutlery, toys, hats, and linoleum, – the mirror image of a department store, in fact, except that everything was sold in dozens or by the gross, and at what today seem absurd prices: a dozen black sateen blouses for 35s. 6d. or the Slenderline corset for "tall, massively proportioned ladies, extremely lissom in appearance" at 59s. 6d. a dozen. Caps for men and boys started off at 4s 11d. a dozen, and the new Leopold skirt grip was a snip at 4s. 6d. for 12.

Another former department store is now transformed into a multi-million-pound business selling workwear: **Alexandra Workwear,** with its headquarters at Patchway, started life as a carving and gilding business in the 1850s in Redcliff Street where Alfred Isaac Davis sold picture frames and his wife worked as a milliner. The story goes that she nagged him into displaying some of her hats in the window, and to Alfred's chagrin, the hats sold better than the frames. So he was persuaded to go into the millinery and hosiery business.

They traded first from 80, Redcliff Street and by 1876 also had a branch in the Hotwell Road. In 1879 he moved to the then fashionable Whiteladies Road, setting up at Nos. 53 and 55 in what was known as the Royal Arcade, a group of shops built by the eccentric architect builder W.J. King, who had also built the Bazaar in Boyce's Avenue.

Alfred Davis set up as The Alexandra Company, named without permission, of course, after the Princess of Wales, later Queen Alexandra, and selling "Nouveautés, Specialités, Modes", since a touch of French never hurt when it came to selling fashion. By 1888 he had sold the Hotwells branch and had acquired No 51, Whiteladies Road as

T.C. Marsh supplied the local gentry in their men's department, pictured in 1922.

The Alexandra sales catalogues were works of art: this 1905 one offered Pains Model hats from 7s 6d; fur stoles from 10s 6d and Donegal tweed at 1s 11½d per yard.

well, and eventually the shop spread, sandwiching the Vittoria public house, to the corner of West Park. The store sold mainly fabrics, hats, children's wear, corsets, haberdashery, furnishing fabrics and bedding, and twice a year issued an elaborate illustrated sale catalogue that was a real work of art. They also offered mourning goods and a "making- up" service on the premises, and advertised "waiting rooms for ladies" on the first floor.

The store soldiered on its respectable way until the Second World War, with Alfred's son and then his grandson Everard Davis in charge. After the war, Whiteladies Road became a less popular shopping centre, over-shadowed by the new Broadmead. Everard Davis responded by closing the department store and moving just two departments to Broadmead. One was fabrics, which went into a shop in Penn Street, and the other, a most unlikely department, overalls, which were sold in St. James Barton. At the time, Everard Davis was thought mad to stake the future on the overalls department, but his incredible foresight paid off, and workwear became the foundation of a new Alexandra empire, now run by the fourth generation, Granville Davis. He retired in 1987, remaining as non-executive chairman.

If a Victorian shopper wanted high-grade fashion, he or she would go to a tailor and outfitter rather than a department store. One firm the men went to was **T.C. Marsh.**

Thomas Culverwell Marsh opened his men's outfitting shop first in Clifton, on the corner of Boyce's Avenue, in 1877. He was a very strict member of the Plymouth Brethren, and a present director of the firm, Mr. John Thorns, who joined in 1922, can remember that Mr. Marsh insisted that the blinds should be brought down in the shop windows on Sundays, to prevent frivolous window-shopping. Mr. Thorns earned £250 a year when he started with the firm.

In 1905, when T.C.Marsh's son Ernest joined the firm, they moved to 90 Whiteladies Road and there traded as children's outfitters specialising in school uniforms. They also became major suppliers of academic gowns and student wear to Bristol University.

Gradually, Marsh's acquired nos. 88,92,92A and B, and established the frontage that exists today, completing the run of buildings by rebuilding when a bomb destroyed no.90. Mr. Thorns recalls when the bomb blew out the men's outfitting department – shirts and pyjamas were hanging on the trees in the street.

This shop from the beginning featured gentlemen's tailoring, and had a large workroom housing two cutters and 30 tailors working flat out to make suits which were delivered, until vans were purchased, on bicycles. At the beginning of Clifton College terms, the shop's entire staff would be roped in to make deliveries.

In the 1930s when the fashion for made-to-measure suits for women came in the firm introduced ladies' tailoring, and during the last war, their expertise was used to make military uniforms. The firm is now scheduled to become a series of minishops, owned by St. Monica's Charity.

Another firm which made its fortune supplying school uniforms is **Steer and Geary** until recently of The Mall, Clifton. This tailoring and outfitting business began as a firm of hosiers and haberdashers in 1836. Its origins are obscure: a Steer owned the shop, next door to a grocer and wine-merchant John Geary, so presumably they joined forces. The turning point came when Clifton College was founded, for from the 1860s onwards,

Steer and Geary supplied the uniforms. The business boasts Victorian photographs dating from 1864, of Clifton masters and pupils, in their cricketing and rugby kit; the latter consisted of striped jerseys worn with bow ties! There is a splendid group photo of Sharpes House in 1877, showing the future Earl Field Marshal Douglas Haig, and on the back is a detailed list of what became of all the boys. One became Keeper of the Crown Jewels, another was Master of the Royal Mint, and another Registrar General, and most exotic of all, one boy, E.W. "Tiger" Lyon was scalped by Indians on his ranch at Arizona.

Above the shop, in living memory, was the tailors' and cutters' room where all the uniforms were made, and on the wall until quite recently was what must be one of Bristol's first inter-com telephones, comprising a mahogany board with a bell, a crank winder, an ear-piece on a cord, and a pointer which was manually moved to the numbers which had to be dialled – a real museum piece. Very recently, the firm merged with John Bedford of nearby Boyce's Avenue, Clifton where the combined business now operates. The shop is now known as Bedford, Steer and Geary.

All that remains of Bristol's once enormous leather trade are three shoe firms and **Thomas Ware,** tanners of Clift House Tannery, Ashton. Bristol had been since medieval times a major centre for the leather trade, with a regular leather market up to the end of the 18th century, and right up to the last war, Bristol firms such as Lindrea and Bracher were big suppliers to the shoe trade.

Thomas Ware started trading in Devon and moved to Clift House, site of a Georgian mansion on the Avon, in 1878. He built a series of tan-pits, drying sheds and warehouses leading down to the water (there is no record of the locals complaining about the smell) and set up to supply leather uppers for boots and shoes, wax kip butts, shoe butts, tongue kips and satin shoulders to the burgeoning Bristol shoe firms, of which only three have survived more than a century.

Shoe-making was one of the last crafts to be affected by the mechanisation of the Industrial Revolution; until the 1860s, dozens of small boot and shoe makers worked from home, selling direct to the public. The organisation of them into factories started in the 1870s, and was then one of the sweated trades, where workers never knew from one day to the next whether there would be any work coming in, and where pay was on starvation level. Not suprisingly, the shoe workers were quick to unionise, and there were several fierce strikes in Bristol and Kingswood in the 1880s and Nineties.

Mass production had to come, and around 1876 to '78, **George Bryant Britton** set up a shoe-making business with his uncle; he built a small factory in Walters Road, Kingswood, and a balance sheet shows, in 1883 copperplate, that the capital stood at £1,100 4s. 11d., and the value of the stock at £1,603. They must have flourished, for by 1886, sales were £24,380.

Even then there was little machinery: most of the work was done by hand, much of it by outworkers. Only four or five boot-makers worked in the factory which contained about 20 sewing machines and three crude presses for cutting out soles and insoles. There were also a dozen clicking boards on which the leather was cut out; what machinery there was was treadle-operated, and gas-driven machines were not installed until the end of the century.

It must be said that boot and shoe-making was at that time a very poorly paid and insecure occupation: in the 1880s and 1890s, anyone walking through the Kingswood streets at night would pass by many a lighted window where bootmakers were catching up on work to be "shopped" the following morning. Workers could not rely on regular daily work, and average earnings of 3s. 6d. a week were common.

However, in 1900, G.B. Britton moved to a larger factory in Lodge Road. The business up to that point had been almost exclusively men's hobnailed boots, first called Dryfoot and then Welshod; they were sold to industrial workers, such as the South Wales tinmen, and when their trade slumped, so did Britton's. The First World War provided a boom; an extension was built to the factory, and Army boots in hundreds of thousands were made from 6.30 a.m. to 9.30 p.m. each working day. But it was not until 1917 that records show the purchase of a "Gimson Consol Laster with knife attachment," followed by three more lasting-machines. For the outworkers, this installation was ominous.

Around this time, production included women's and children's hobnailed boots, made with rows of bright hobs, known as "nuggets", on the soles. In 1915, a pair of child's hobnailed boots with iron heels and toe plates – these boots were meant to last – cost 2s. 11d.

After the First World War, there was a boom as shops restocked, and then came a slump and a huge drop in the price of leather. During this critical time, one of the firm's best markets, Ireland, was lost because of the setting up of the Irish Free State trade barriers, and, in 1929, G.B. Britton died, in harness. He had been both Lord Mayor and a Bristol M.P. simultaneously, a Sunday school superintendent, and a boss who worked alongside his men in overalls.

After his death the outworkers finally went, as slowly the factory was completely mechanised. Lighter footwear was designed – and then again war intervened. The factory was requisitioned for aircraft production, and the machinery had to be moved to another local firm. Old employees remember a spectacular aerial dog-fight above the factory, when nearly 50 German bombers were routed by a squadron of Hurricanes. Several German machine gun bullets were found embedded in the roof the next day. After the war, the firm re-established itself as the successful one we know today, with a nation-wide business.

Another shoe firm going strong a century ago was **Lennards,** founded by five Leicester brothers, Samuel, John, William, Barry and Thomas Lennard in the 1860s. Thomas, later Sir Thomas, started trading with a chain delightfully named the Public Benefit Boot Company. It had several branches in the West Country but business was best of all in Bristol, where there was a branch in the High Street in the 1880s. In 1889, Sir Thomas, who visited every one of his branches individually, travelling 20,000 miles a year by rail, decided to make Bristol his headquarters by setting up a warehouse in Temple Street and a head office in The Triangle, roughly on the site where Gillow's is today. It was known to everyone as Lennard's Corner, and a whole rank of houses was demolished to make way for it. The building was destroyed in the Blitz.

In Bristol the business was still known as the Public Benefit Boot Company, providing "Benefit Boots, good and cheap" until early in this century, when the name changed to Lennards Ltd. In 1938 the headquarters was transferred to Staple Hill, where it stayed

Above: Lennard's Corner, a famous Bristol landmark at Queens Road, seen in wartime, before the building was blitzed.

Below: No automation at the Brooks Laundry wash-house, seen in the 1920s.

until 1973, when the firm was bought by Great Universal Stores, and the headquarters moved to Leicester.

A wonderful example of how to adapt and survive comes from another shoe firm, which started life as **Stubbs and Burt** in the 1870s. Frederick Burt started shoe-making in the 1850s, but later joined Ralph Stubbs and his son in St. Nicholas Street, and in 1895 they styled themselves "anatomical bootmakers", for they made surgical boots as well as riding boots, bespoke shoes, ceremonial footwear and leggings. The premises were opposite the fruit and vegetable market and most of the actual shoe and boot-making was carried out in the homes of outworkers, who came in once a week for instructions and materials. The firm made court shoes – the slip-ons with buckles worn by The Lord Mayor and the Sheriff – and boots for the Bristol mounted police.

In 1940 the shop was completely destroyed by incendiary bombs, and all the custom-ers' lasts, patterns and measures, and some 70 years of books and records were lost. The firm found a new home in St. Stephen's Street, at the ornate No.17, where they remained selling hand-made bespoke shoes, until 1966. By 1968, when the firm moved to Kingswood, it was realised that selling hand-made shoes was no longer a way of making a living.

The change of direction came from a memory that in 1946, a Miss Valerie East, an ice-skater, had come to the firm for a pair of skating-boots. So they started making them at 7 guineas for a made-to-measure pair, and were soon besieged with orders, which led to Stubbs and Burt being prime movers in bringing an ice-rink to Bristol. The skating-boots were such a success that they started making ready-to-wear ones, as well as bespoke ones for world champions. Also back in 1953, Arsenal footballer Wally Barnes had asked them to make him a pair of lightweight football boots in black chrome leather. They obliged and soon most of the 1st, 2nd, and 3rd Division teams were wearing the Wally Barnes boot, and from these new beginnings, Stubbs and Burt became Stubert, makers of sports footwear that is exported all over the world.

The invention of dry-cleaning, by a Frenchman called Jolly-Bellin in 1849, when he accidentally spilled turpentine onto a tablecloth, must have come as a boon and a bless-ing, for Victorian outer clothing was undoubtedly smelly. The shrinkable fabrics could not be washed, only sponged, and moreover the new artificial dyes would have run. Only underwear could be properly washed in soap and water.

There were laundries around, of course, before the invention of dry cleaning, and several very old Bristol laundries closed down in the past ten years. The one survivor is **Brooks,** who like most of them, began as dyers: dyeing clothes black for mourning, or to give them a new lease of life, was big business. The dyers also refurbished clothes and sold trimmings, and this was what Alfred Brooks did at his business in Castle Street and later, Broadmead. The firm was established in 1819 as May and Collins. Mr. Collins was the uncle of Alfred Brooks, ninth son of a dyer who could not find any more room for his progeny in his own business. So Alfred came to Bristol and eventually bought out his uncle and set up on his own in 1862.

He offered "the dyeing and curling of ostrich feathers for the ladies of Bristol", and called himself a "London" dyer and cleaner, later offering specialised services such as shirt laundering, glazing of chintz and the Victorian equivalent of blanket re-conditioning.

By the 1870s he was advertising the revolutionary new French process, *nettoyage à sec,* which entailed taking the garments to pieces, cleaning them in spirit and reassembling them, and he cashed in on the craze for stiff collars, offering a service which resulted in 40,000 a week being processed.

By the end of the century, Brooks added hat renovation and carpet cleaning to their repertoire. They were one of the first firms to go over entirely to motor vans, as early as 1912. There were branches, too, after 1870, at Clifton and Weston-super-Mare, and land was acquired at Ashley Vale, their present headquarters, now covering three and a half acres. Alfred Brooks lived long enough to see all this happen before his death, aged 86, in 1927.

Right up to the Second World War, the laundry business was very labour-intensive, with hundreds of women working over steaming tubs, turning mangles, and finishing the clothes by hand. People went on sending their personal laundry in every Monday until the Sixties, when automatic washing machines and synthetic fabrics made home laundering much easier. Nowadays the bulk of the business, apart from the drycleaning, is leasing and laundering hotel linen, and workwear. Simon Brooks, the present chairman, is the fourth generation to hold that position.

5 – Home Sweet Home.

The scene is Brazil in 1881. John Charles Morgan, a diplomat who had retired from the consular service, went out for an evening's gambling at cards, and won a considerable sum. But his debtor was unable to pay him. Instead he gave John Morgan a secret formula that would make his fortune in a whole new Victorian industry: home-making.

A tall story? Yet John Charles Morgan came to Bristol in 1882 and used his secret formula to set up a business that is going to this day. This was the bizarre beginning of **Purimachos** Fire Cement, a compound for mending cracked grates. It was an instant success in an age when smoking grates were the bane of the housemaid's life.

John Morgan set up his factory in St. Philips, and was soon selling his product not just to private homes, but to gas works, power stations and steel works in Britain, France, Belgium, Russia, Sweden, Canada and the United States. He had found a way of bonding joints that would not lead to cracking in extreme heat (the name Purimachos is from the Greek, and means fire-fighting). The new product superseded fire-clay for use in coating kilns and furnaces in the steel, glassmaking and pottery industries.

In the home, housewives and maids found additional uses for the fire cement: they cleaned saucepans with it, and knives, and used it to clean dirty hands and greasy sinks.

Purimachos fire cement was used in the humblest cottages and in the highest homes in the land. The Clerk of the Works at Balmoral swore by it in 1932 and revealed: "It was first used here in Queen Victoria's time, upwards of 45 years ago, and has been in constant use ever since". Purimachos got a Royal Charter in 1919.

The company grew so much that in 1923 it had to move to larger premises in Waterloo Road, its present site. In 1934 there was a macabre scandal when workmen excavating a yard found human remains, and the police were called in. But then a 1763 tombstone and several coffins were discovered and the firm found that they had built their new headquarters on a private 18th century burial ground.

The advent of central heating in the 1950s made cracked grates less common, so the firm diversified into a boat company which built motor launches and later racing dinghies and, in 1972, they bought out their main fire cement rival: in 1986 they launched a range of DIY products. There is still a Morgan in charge, James, the great grandson of the founder.

The hunger of Victorian Bristolians for a home of their own created a lot of business for various people: timber merchants, brick makers, builders, glaziers, paint manufacturers and estate agents. But first the prospective owner had to raise the money to buy his house.

Bristol's own building society, The **Bristol, West of England and South Wales Permanent Benefit Building Society,** was founded on June 11th, 1850, by the leading business and professional men of the city. The first Board consisted of 15 members with John Lucas as chairman, and in its early days faced strong competition, since some 200 building societies had been set up nationally between 1845 and 1865. But by the end of its 10th year, Bristol and West had accumulated receipts of more than £46,000, advances over £25,000, and, besides paying interest and bonuses to its inves-

Builders John Perkins & Son started out in Redland as well-sinkers and plasterers: this was the well-boring equipment and the staff at the turn of the century.

tors, had accumulated a Guarantee Fund of £550.

The figures are minute by modern standards, but in 1865 a small house could be bought for about £100 – the average wage of the working man was less than fifteen shillings a week.

Bristol and West had always had its head office in the commercial heart of Bristol, first in Small Street and then in St. Stephen's Street where they stayed until 1939. Their subsequent head offices, near St. Stephens Church and now at Broad Quay were both built by Cowlins, another subject in this book.

In 1876, receipts passed the £1 million mark, and in 1881 they opened a Current Deposit Department which operated rather like a bank, except that there were no overdrafts. Even in the early years, building societies were faced with the vexed question of income tax, which was resolved in 1894 when Somerset House agreed that investors and borrowers should be exempt from income tax on interest received.

The Society coped with a housing boom after the First World War, when Bristol had 36,000 new homes built, of which 20,000 were private houses, and then with another burst of building and re-building after the Second World War. By the 1970s, Bristol and West had become national, and at present ranks as the 12th largest building society in the country, with 165 offices and assets of around £3,000 million.

In 1987, building societies were given wider powers. Ever in the forefront of activities, Bristol & West soon announced a tie up with a leading stockbroking firm, and the acquisition of a number of West Country firms of estate agents. Its current television advertising campaign features Joan Collins, of 'Dynasty' soap opera fame – a far cry from the staid image presented in its early publicity.

The building firm which did most to change the Victorian skyline of the city was **Cowlins,** started by William Cowlin in Milk Street in 1834. In 1865 he was joined by his son, and from then on, dozens of important public buildings, as well as thousands of private homes and shops were their responsibility: they built the City Art Gallery and Museum, the Wills building for the University, the W.D. and H.O. Wills factory in Bedminster, the tobacco warehouses, the old telephone exchange, Clifton College Chapel, Sea Mills Garden suburb, the Bristol Brewery and part of the B.R.I., as well as undertaking dozens of church restoration schemes. They built abroad as well, at the turn of the century, in Jamaica, Brazil and Canada, and went on changing the face of Bristol with new cinemas, banks and factories, and later this century built landmarks like Electricity House in the centre and the new Council House. At the same time they expanded to add an estate agent's department and a decorating department in Clifton, and in 1915 went in for furniture warehousing.

An admirer of the firm in the 1890s said: "In their decorative work they have acted as pioneers for the trade of the West of England in the practical application of that great aesthetic revival which has done so much to improve both the exterior and the interior of English building." He meant Bristol neo-Gothic.

Another building firm going strong in the 1860s was that of **John Perkins,** the perfect example of the Victorian self-made man. He lived near Berkeley in Gloucestershire, where his father had a small-holding, and was educated at Thornbury Grammar School. His father wanted him to work on the small-holding, but the boy refused and ran away from home. He came to Bristol and started working for a builder, as a brickie at first, and soon learned the trade and got on.

In 1862 he left to set up his own business in Lower Redland Road, and the family legend is that he raised the money by answering an advertisement in the local paper saying that if John Perkins contacted a solicitor, he would learn something to his advantage. He did, got a legacy, and started his firm as a cornice-maker and well-borer – a strange combination, but both were in demand in Victorian Redland and Clifton in the 1860s, when new houses were going up at a furious pace, and where Bristol Waterworks had not yet provided mains water.

He also built several villas in Redland, and fathered six sons, five of whom joined the business. On his death his son Audley took over, and the company was incorporated in 1906. Audley Perkins was a great entrepreneur, and the firm began to get contracts all over the country for building and civil engineering work. They built the pool at Weston-super-Mare in the 1920s, were early contractors to Shell-Mex, and did huge construction work for them at Ellesmere Port; at one time the firm had branches there and in London, and employed 9,000 men during the Second World War, when they were building refineries for the war effort. They also worked on extending the Manchester Ship Canal in 1931, and laid the main services for the Portway when it was built in 1935.

Locally, they went in for difficult projects, like re-siting the famous equestrian statue by Rysbrack, in Queen Square, when the road was driven through in 1937, and they kept up their cornice-work: Perkins did the alteration to the Merchant Venturers' house in The Promenade, when two houses were converted into one, and decorated the ceiling of Lloyds Bank in Corn Street.

Audley Perkins was succeeded by his son John Howard, and the present managing director is his son David, who, like his father and grandfather before him, was Bristol President of the Building Employers' Confederation. Their present headquarters in Belmont Street, Easton, has historic interest, too, for it incorporates the remains of Easton Manor, a house where Queen Anne supposedly stayed.

As well as the big builders, there were small firms which served the house-proud Victorians. They needed house decorators, so in the mid-century, **Albert Mogford** set up business with his sons at 140, Whiteladies Road in a shop selling paints and artists' materials. One of his sons, another Albert, had become more interested in being an artist than a decorator, and, being no businessman, was not a financial success, and the shop closed down. But Albert Mogford senior moved to Westbury Hill to live, and persuaded his younger son William in the 1890s to open an ironmongery shop at 2, Westbury Hill, and to build up a decorating trade. William was the grandfather of the present owner, E.W. Mogford, who still runs exactly the same kind of business, with general contracting work thrown in.

William soon left his wife in charge of the shop and went out on decorating jobs with his men. All the steps and ladders and cans of paint were pushed about on handcarts, and they travelled miles to the various big houses of the day. In fact William met his wife when he was doing a painting job at Leigh Court, where she was the head cook.

His son trained as a solicitor, but found it too tame, so he too joined the family firm, whose business at that time included bicycle repairs, milk churn soldering, and grinding; the business even had its own forge. The present owner was born over the shop, and can remember that in the Thirties they stayed open from 8 a.m. to 8 p.m. and 9.30 p.m. on Saturdays. He was apprenticed as a plumber, on a starting wage of 5s. a week, going up by 2s. 6d. a year to the age of 20, when his pay went up to a magnificent £1 a week. He was annoyed to see in his father's books that he was charged out at 1s. an hour to the customers. The prices to the customers were amazing by modern standards: in 1919 a customer had a bedroom ceiling whitened, the walls stripped and re-papered and the woodwork painted, all for 30s.

When 18th century Bristolians wanted paint or glass they went to **John Hall,** a colourman and glazier in Broadmead. He was a country boy who came from Dorset to Bristol in the 1780s to be appreticed, Bristol being then the main city for glass of all kinds, especially window panes, which were exported to America in huge quantities. During his apprenticeship, John Hall travelled all over the country on contracts for his master, and saw fine 18th century taste in decorating and furnishing in the great houses.

On the last day of his apprenticeship in 1788, his father, a farmer, presented him with a legacy, to set him up as a glazier. John Hall soon realised that he could usefully supply putty and paint as well, and made it up himself, by grinding and blending the colours and mixing them with varnish and turpentine. The painter would put on several coats, rubbing down after each and finishing with a coat of varnish.

But it was as a glazier that the firm was famous in the last century; John Hall imported, processed and distributed glass all over the country, supplied stained glass for houses and churches, and opened a warehouse in London. Competition in the glass trade after 1918 drove the firm to specialise in cut and embossed glass, leaded lights and mirrors, and in 1920, the firm pioneered the first ready mixed gloss paint, Brolac, and in 1927 established a new factory near Whitchurch. Brolac at that time was made with a water and steam resistant oil from the Tung tree, known as Chinese Wood Oil, and it became popular after the then novel idea of a nation-wide advertising campaign.

The company had been formed into a private limited company in 1897 by John Wesley Hall, grandson of the founder, with his three brothers Alfred, Alec and Samuel, and his eldest son John, and there was a Hall in the business right up to the 1960s. In 1929 they started a cellulose factory near Albert Road, St. Philips, in order to cater for the growing market in aircraft and other industrial finishes, an expertise which paid off in the Second World War. The main general offices in Broadmead, which had been there for 150 years, were flattened in the Blitz, and all the company's records were lost. In 1954, John Hall merged with Jenson Nicholas, and that company merged with the Berger Group. John Hall operated independently until 1983, when Berger re-organised, and the ancient name disappeared.

Another man dealing with glass, but in a very different way, was **Joseph Bell,** who designed and made hundreds of the stained glass windows in Bristol's Victorian houses, and in the city's churches.

He started life as a pottery painter in Stoke, and set up in Wilson Street, Bristol in 1840 in a humble way, painting house-names and numbers and designing and making decorative glass for doors and windows. But his forte was ecclesiastical stained glass, and from 1858, when he moved to College Green, he worked on churches all over Bristol and the West Country, either making new windows or restoring old ones. When work was being done on Bristol Cathedral's windows after the last war, the craftsmen found that much of what they thought was medieval glass was, in fact, skilful restoration work by Joseph Bell. His work can still be seen in cathedrals at Bristol, Gloucester, Wells and in St. Mary Redcliffe, and he was one of the first of the Victorian glass workers to interest himself in the new glass-making techniques which produced "muff" glass, the nearest thing to the long-lost craft of medieval glass. He left several note-books full of sketches showing designs for windows, coats of arms, memorials, and little drawings of church architecture, and lines from poems.

His kiln long survived him: it was moved from College Green up to the present work-shop at 68 Park Street, where it was still in use in 1962. Joseph Bell's son Frederick sold the business to Arnold Robinson in 1923, and his son Geoffrey carries on much the same craft as the founder, mainly working in churches, and sometimes restoring Joseph Bell's work. It is the third oldest firm of its kind in the country.

Timber was one of Bristol's earliest imports, used mainly for house building when Bristol's houses were all timber-framed, but also for furniture, boat-building and, in the 19th century, for the railways and the factories of the Industrial Revolution.

The oldest surviving timber firm is **Jonathan Hill,** now owned by **Wickham Norris.** One of the spin-offs of the slave trade was the importation into Bristol of mahogany, which came at first from the West Indies. One of the earliest mahogany importers in Bristol was Thomas Woodward, who started his business in 1750; when he died in 1799, it passed to James Hill who, with his son Jonathan, rebuilt the premises in Merchant Street. Jonathan Hill II was the first timber merchant in the city to use a horizontal log saw, and his two sons carried on the business until 1924, when Wickham Norris took it over.

This firm had been started in 1840 by Jessie Heaven, near Temple Gate; he joined forces with F.W.Wickham, who later became sole owner and took on Robert Norris in 1865. Steam-driven machinery was coming into the timber yards, and Wickham and Norris installed theirs in 1872. This plant would have been used to cut logs and baulks of timber which before then had been cut over a saw pit by hand, one man at the top of the baulk and the other down below, pulling the saw up and down. In 1878 they started to make mouldings and floorings by machine, and installed what was probably the first drying kiln in Bristol, for timber seasoning. They were pioneers, too, in being the first timber firm to install electricity in 1905, and in 1923, they bought the first petrol-driven articulated timber lorry. And you can tell from their number how early they were in having the telephone. It was Bristol 15.

In 1905 the whole concern was moved to Wapping Dock; by the First World War, they were contracted to the Admiralty, and shrewdly bought all the remaining Admiralty stock when the war ended.

Clarks Wood Co. Ltd. is another timber firm dating from the 18th century – founded in 1797. But sadly, all records were lost in a move from Bedminster to Silverthorne Lane twenty years ago. All that is known is that the firm originated in a sawmill in Bedminster and that one of the family, William Clark, was hanged for taking part in the Bristol Riots, when he helped destroy the Bristol Gaol and Bridewell. In 1832

Telegrams—"ROBBINS, BRISTOL."   *Telephone No.* 404

ROBBINS LIMITED,

Imperial Saw Mills, Cumberland Road, BRISTOL,

. . MANUFACTURERS OF . .

Doors, Sashes & Frames, Dressers, Kitchen Cupboards, &c.

Staircases & Bay Windows a Speciality.

Builders' Mouldings & Handrails,

Newels and Balusters $\left(\begin{array}{c}\text{Round or}\\\text{Square Turned}\end{array}\right).$

IMPORTERS OF FOREIGN DOORS.

Largest Bent Timber Manufacturers in the West of England to the Coach & Motor Trades.

WHEELS, SHAFTS, SPOKES, FELLOES & BOARDS OF EVERY DESCRIPTION.

Above: Robbins, the timber firm were selling bent timber to the car trade by 1913.
Below: How timber was delivered to Clarks Wood, Bedminster, about 1901.

he and four others were executed in front of a large crowd of spectators outside the Gaol, and contemporary accounts identified him as the nephew of a Mr. Clark who owned a sawmill. At any rate, *Mathews' Directory* for 1818 lists a Samuel Clark, chair and timber dealer, North Street, Bedminster.

Bristol's suburbs had begun to expand by 1858 when **Thomas Christopher May** and **Robert Hassell** started up as timber, mahogany and slate merchants in Cumberland Road, at a time when the building trade was hungry for materials. Little is known about Hassell, but T.C. May is known to be the son of a Non-Conformist who was apprenticed at the age of ten or twelve to a timber merchant. By the age of 16, he was travelling in Gloucestershire and Somerset on horseback, selling his firm's goods. Eventually he bought his master's business and set up on his own. The business he bought, John Salmon and Co., dated back earlier than any other timber firm in the city. Many of May's first contracts were with railway companies, and he did so well that a branch was opened in West Hartlepool in 1863, and ten years later, a London office was set up. In its first 20 years, May and Hassell became one of the largest timber firms in the country.

The founder had three sons to follow him: Arthur, a keen huntsman and secretary of the Berkeley Hunt, who used to come into the office with his hunting clothes covered with a huge mackintosh to avoid embarassment; Frank, a solicitor, and Howard, who managed the Poole office, opened in 1886. He was a keen musician and conducted the Bournemouth Choral Society; his other love was driving a four-in-hand, or failing that, a penny-farthing bicycle. He won the tandem competition at the Bath and West Show, and was the May who set up a trade link with Russia, having visited the country after the Revolution, in the 1920s.

Howard May was the last of the family to be chairman; he retired in 1937, and since then the company has expanded, with sawmills and stocks at 30 depots throughout the country. In the Second World War, when timber supplies were taken over by the Government, May and Hassell invested in 5,000 acres of farmland, and eggs went on sale at the Bedminster office which they had moved to after being bombed out of Cumberland Road. They stayed in Bedminster until 1971, when they moved to their present headquarters at Avonmouth.

In the 1860s and 70s, vast amounts of Scandinavian whitewood poles were coming into Bristol Docks. They were imported because of the housebuilding boom's demand for scaffolding poles. A familiar figure on the dock would be **Alfred Beer,** who stood at the foot of the gangplank to watch out for the most perfect lengths of pole. He wanted them for his ladder-making business which he had started in North Street, Bedminster, in 1869. Beer was the son of an Almondsbury wheelwright who used to make ladders from the spare spokes of cartwheels. Alfred developed the idea, making ladders, flag-staffs, and supplying the building trade, the telegraph service, and the fire service in the last century. During the First World War, the firm made ammunition boxes, and between the wars, when Bristolians were anxious to hear the new BBC radio service, put up on thousands of city chimneys long poles, with wire cages on the end, to improve reception.

In the Second World War they made ladders for Civil Defence and the Auxiliary Fire

Service and, when peace came, private and civic rejoicing was signalled by flags run up on Beer's flagpoles; the one by Neptune's statue is their's. Their ladders are still made in the traditional way, despite the advent of modern machinery. Rule of thumb and a keen eye are still an essential part of the ladder-maker's skill, says Alfred Beer's grandson, John Bradshaw.

Another grandson in the timber trade is Brian **Robbins,** whose grandfather Frank came from Devizes in 1881 to join a partnership in a sawing and planing mill in Cumberland Road, where they also produced bent timber and made carriages and coaches. May and Hassell were next-door, and the whole area was known as Baltic or Canada Wharf, after the countries where the timber came from. Baker and Robbins operated the only saw mill on the wharf, and so did work for their rivals; the saw mill was operated by a beam engine, and conveyor belts removed the waste, which was used to fire the boiler that provided steam for the engine. Frank Robbins was a skilled engineer, and a model of the beam engine he used can be seen in the Industrial Museum.

Frank was followed by his son Harold, who trained for a year with May and Hassell and for a year with a timber farmer in Devon; in the age of the motor car, the coach-building side of the business declined, but the joinery side boomed, especially in the sale of panelled doors. By the First World War the main need was for wooden ammunition boxes. Next came the building boom of the Thirties. This was the age of the "journey" traveller, who sold Robbins wares all over the South-West, Wales, the Midlands, and even as far as the Channel Islands. Cheap joinery had become available, but the firm refused to compromise on standards, and their joinery shop was carried by other departments until it was finally closed down by Hitler's bombs. Firewatching in such an inflammable business became the rule, and precious tea and sugar rations were locked in the company's fire-proof strong room!

Robbins' main war work was to produce English oak and ash battens and Douglas fir bends for the manufacture of Carley floats for the Navy. The founder's grandson, Brian Robbins, started work in 1944, but when the war ended, tenancy problems arose because all the land was leasehold and the Port of Bristol wanted to terminate the lease. The firm went through a bad patch in the Fifties. The end of horse-drawn vehicles, the end of Utility bentwood style furniture and major changes in caravan design all left them behind the times, and by 1957 they faced the prospect of voluntary liquidation. But Brian Robbins replaced the outdated machinery – the workshops were not even using electricity until 1951 – and the firm's fortunes were turned round; a new office block was built in 1969, and work was diversified to include materials for boat-builders. The DIY revolution was also under way. In 1977, Brian's daughter Hilary joined the firm, and two years later came the eviction order, because Baltic Wharf was needed for houses. So the firm moved to Bedminster in 1981, and their hundredth year in Cumberland Road was marked by a clearance sale.

The other big need of the building trade was bricks: Georgian freestone had been abandoned in favour of Victorian brick – and there was a Bristol brick-maker to supply them.

The **Cattybrook Brick Works** came into existence because of Brunel's plan to construct a railway line linking Bristol with a ferry service that crossed the Severn estuary to Wales. In 1858 Brunel instructed his resident engineer Charles Richardson to drive the Patchway Tunnel. The clay found there in excavations was removed, and since it was the habit of the day for the contractor to make a few bricks for himself, Mr. Richardson did so, and was impressed by the hardness and soundness of the result. When the line was finished, he investigated the matter more deeply, and satisfied himself that "an article could be produced from this clay which was superior to any made in the neighbourhood and not excelled by any in the country."

So in 1860 he acquired Cattybrook Farm near Almondsbury, and built a small works, which was in action by 1864. Clay was mixed with water by a horse circling round a pug mill, then put into moulds, and a miniature railway system was set up for transport.

In 1863, the directors of GWR decided to tunnel under the Severn, and again the engineer for the work was Charles Richardson, who began the hazardous task in 1874. After various troubles with flooding, the tunnel was completed in 1886, having used 19 million Cattybrook bricks. It was the making of the company and paid for modernisation. By 1900 Cattybrook, today owned by Ibstock Building Products Ltd., had 21 kilns and began selling all over the country and even to the West Indies; before the First World War, the works employed 250 men and made 20 million bricks a year, many of them destined for buildings in Bristol. Boom times are back: the current fashion for decorative brickwork on new buildings continues to keep the Cattybrook works busy.

Another group which did very well in Bristol's Victorian housing boom were the estate agents, auctioneers and appraisers, like the firm of Tricks and Wallop, now known as **Osmond Tricks,** set up in St. Nicholas Street in 1858.

William Tricks, great-great-grandfather of the present principal, George Tricks, took advantage of the boom in trade from the 1850's to service the new industries, shops and housing springing up. He was joined, by his son Charles in 1875, and he was succeeded by his son Frederick, who was devoted to the Prince's Theatre in Park Row; he was secretary to the theatre in the time of James Macready Chute, and became a director. He had great plans for the rebuilding and restoring of the Prince's, after its destruction in 1941, but died before his dream could be achieved.

The firm had another theatre connection: in 1940 Dennis Tricks, also a director of the Prince's, purchased the Theatre Royal in King Street on behalf of a philanthropic client who wished to remain anonymous. This rescued the building, which at that time was destined to be turned into a banana warehouse. Thus the finest 18th century theatre in the country was saved to become a home for the Bristol Old Vic.

Another Tricks actually trod the boards. Nancy, daughter of Frederick, was a popular soprano and the leading lady in many amateur productions.

In 1968 the firm amalgamated with the auctioneers, Victor Osmond, who had been in business in the city for more than half a century, first at Small Street and then in Queen Square.

The modern firm of **Hoddell Pritchard** has its origins in two very old firms: Alonzo Dawes and Hoddell started in Clevedon in 1865, and Pritchards can trace their roots back to at least 1785.

In the late 18th century, when houses were going up rapidly, a John Alexander set up

in Broadmead as a broker and auctioneer, getting his licence in 1785. His first deal was the sale of William Russell's brewery and effects at Temple Back, and an advertisement of the period shows him selling "A messuage or dwelling house situated at Lower Church Lane in the parish of St. Michael." Estate agent's prose was around even then, for he described it as having "an extensive prospect of the whole city and country round, and well worth £14 p.a. clear of taxes." After several moves, the firm ended up in Corn Street, and merged with Pritchards in 1910.

The other half of the story begins in Clevedon in 1865 where Alonzo Dawes had a strange combination of trades; he was an auctioneer, valuer, and coal and salt merchant. He also helped to form Clevedon's Fire Brigade. In 1896 he was joined by his son Edward, who had the idea of opening a saleroom, which still exists, in Clevedon.

Their main rivals were the Bristol firm of Hoddells, founded by a surveyor, James Hoddell, who began his practice in 1874, styling himself an architect as well as auctioneer, estate agent and coal merchant. He designed villas in Clevedon besides several houses in Bristol, including 1-9 Pembroke Vale, Clifton. James Hoddell's son Herbert succeeded him, and his son Robert married Margery Dawes, making another merger inevitable. Another firm which joined up was that of George Nichols Hunt and Co., who had the house at Quay Head with the s.s. *Demerara* figurehead outside – sadly it disintegrated when it was taken down.

Pritchards and Alonzo Dawes and Hoddell merged in 1982, and later became a member of the General Accident Group, operating as Hoddell Pritchard Ltd.

As the name suggests, **Lalonde** is of French origin. In the early 1870s, Emile and Mary Lalonde left France in one of their family's ships for Southampton; there they sold the vessel and made their way to Weston-super-Mare. With six children and in straitened circumstances, Emile started teaching French, while his son Emile Gustave went to work for Samuel Norton, auctioneer and valuer of West Street. In 1886 the younger Emile married Kitty Norton and was made a partner; his brother Septimus joined him in 1894, and a third brother, William, who had opened a furniture shop, married into an estate agent's family. So between the four of them they had in one family an auctioneer, valuer, furniture remover and estate agent. In 1898 they all joined forces and opened their new firm, Lalonde Bros and Parham, in Bristol.

In the early years they were also a big removals firm, using "horseless wagons, steam road locomotives and road trains," which were a series of three linked wagons, pulled by a traction engine, but on roads, not rails. They claimed in 1908 that this new method of transport "effects great economy over Horses or Rail, combined with Comfort and Expedition. Our vans are built after our own designs, embodying the Latest Improvements to ensure easy riding and safe transit of the most delicate furniture."

In the Thirties they began to handle the selling of the new housing estates which mushroomed in the city, and in 1938 they took on the first outside partner, setting a trend for the future. Since 1960 they have handled many of the big office developments in the central area of the city, including Avon House, Froomsgate House and Templeway House. With the growth of large agency groups, the residential side now operate as Prudential Residential Services, and the commercial business is conducted by Chesterton Lalonde.

Above: Bristol & West's entire staff, all ten of them, posed for the photographer in 1900. Today there are over 1,400 employees.

Below: Alonzo Dawes (wearing the top hat) pictured in 1884.

Edward T. Parker who established his firm of chartered surveyors in Broad Street in 1879, deserves to be remembered for another reason: he was the founder of Bristol Dogs' Home.

The story goes that one snowy day, Edward T. Parker came to his office and found a stray dog sitting on his doorstep. He took it in, realised there was not much he could do for the dog himself, and had the idea of starting a dogs' home. So he set up a committee of local businessmen to raise funds and find a building, and in 1887, the Bristol Home for Lost and Starving Dogs in Albert Road was opened. Edward T. Parker was its first secretary and treasurer, and there has been a member of the Parker family on the committee ever since.

The present principal of the firm, Keith Whitehead, says that his first job on joining the company in 1948 was to file correspondence about the Dogs' Home and bequests to it, and to take details of poor people deserving of free dog licences; he also had to collect biscuits and tins of dog food for the doggies' Christmas dinner!

Edward T. Parker, who was a keen sailor and a friend of the millionaire grocery-chain owner Sir Thomas Lipton, employed as his office-boy a certain Herbert Ricketts, who eventually became the first person outside London to become a Fellow of the Institute of Estate Agents and Surveyors. He was made a partner, and the firm passed first to Edward's son Leslie and then to his grandson Norman Parker. The firm split into two companies in 1982, one half trading as estate agents and surveyors, the other as auctioneers and valuers.

When **Charles Joseph Hole** started his estate agency business at 1, Queens Road, in 1867, his main business was rent collecting – in Victorian times it was much more common to rent than to buy. He used a team of rent collectors to go round from house to house, and they also collected ground rents. He managed properties for landlords, seeing to the lettings, repairs and so on, a function the firm only stopped carrying out in 1986. The last rents were collected in 1981.

C.J. Hole passed the business on to his two sons Charles Edward and John, and the business moved to 78, Park Street. The brothers were very different: John was shy while Charles had a fierce temper, and at some stage they had a terrible quarrel, and only spoke to one another via messengers. It was not ended until they shook hands over the smoking ruins of their office, after it had been bombed in 1940. The firm moved to 82 and then 84, Park Street, and each time, dozens of heavy old ledgers had to be installed in the basements. A secretary who worked there before the last war recalls the problems with rats and mice, and was not reassured when a Rodent Inspector from the Corporation revealed that the mice had ancient runs down Park Street to the warehouses in the Docks, through all the old cellars.

After the war, Charles Hole sold out to an army captain Roland Francis-Fisher, who ran the office like a regiment, and John's son Stephen, after trying the family firm, bought a car spare parts business, and with John Hole's death the family connection ended. The firm, part of Hanover Druce, now has 15 branches and specialises in estate agency and surveying.

Sponsorship is nothing new: this is the cover of the 1927-28 brochure for the Duck Son & Pinker series of concerts at the Colston Hall.

6 – Leisure and luxury.

The rise of an affluent middle class in Bristol after the Industrial Revolution, added to the particular bent of Bristolians for trade, ensured that there was plenty of spending money about in the city for one section of society, at least.

What did they spend it on? On ample supplies of food and clothing, of course, but also on jewels, parties at local hotels, photography, fine art, sport and music. Music was a passion in Victorian Bristol and every self-respecting middle class family owned a piano or harmonium and piles of sheet music for songs. They were keen concert and theatre-goers, too.

They could have bought the piano from **Duck Son and Pinker,** who started up in Bath in 1848 and opened a Bristol branch in 1886. William Duck was a talented concertina player who joined forces with piano tuner Thomas Pinker in 1878. The Bristol branch was first at 13, Queen's Road and later at grand premises at 1, Royal Promenade, where they had a lofty showroom on three floors, all crammed with pianos, harmoniums and organs. In 1911 a limited company was formed, with the famous Bristol organist George Riseley as a director. Branches were opened at Swansea, Hereford and Swindon, and their success enabled the firm to become sponsors of concerts – the idea is not a new one.

After the First World War, Duck Son and Pinker sponsored International Celebrity Concerts at the Colston Hall for many years, selling tickets on a subscription basis. The programme of the 1927-28 season, for example, for which "all corners of the globe had been scoured to obtain the greatest Artists and most brilliant exponents of the Art of Music", offered the farewell appearance of pianist Pachman, the cellist Suggia, Elena Gerhardt with Alfred Cortot, an evening of grand opera with the London Symphony Orchestra conducted by Thomas Beecham, a recital by Backhaus, and a Strauss evening – seven concerts which, in the stalls, cost £2. 0s. 6d. for the series. The concerts were managed by Charles Lockier, who took them over himself when he parted from the firm after a policy agreement.

The palatial Queen's Road premises were blitzed during the Second World War, as was the shop in the High Street, and "Ducks" had to find a temporary home in four different shops. None of them was suitable and they told their Bristol customers in 1963 that they would have to leave the city for the time being. They promised to be back, and in 1975 found a new home in the Lower Arcade.

Another Victorian passion was photography; for their earliest equipment they would have gone to **Husbands,** on the corner of Denmark Street, still in the premises in which the firm was founded in 1762 by Thomas Husbands, who made surveying instruments. He also made telescopes and microscopes in his top floor workshop, and discovered that the lenses could also be used to magnify writing, so he went into the spectacle business with his three sons. Thomas died in 1778; afterwards his sons had a huge quarrel and split up. One went to Southampton, another to Australia where he evidently flourished, for there is a Victorian photograph of his premises, a corrugated hut with "also in Bristol" on it, and the third son, Henry, kept the Bristol shop. He

EYESIGHT
AND
SPECTACLES
BY
H. HUSBANDS & SONS, M.B.O.A.,
(Members of the British Optical Association).

QUALIFIED OPTICIANS.

SPECTACLE MAKERS.

8, ST. AUGUSTINE'S PARADE.
Works—25 & 26, Denmark Street,
BRISTOL.

ESTABLISHED 1762.

Fry Bros., Printers, Broad Quay, Bristol, 1897.

"Information respecting Eyesight and Spectacles", a give-away booklet for customers, written by Husbands in 1897. The cover shows their Denmark Street shop, the present home.

expanded the optician's side of the business – and then came the invention of photography.

Henry Husbands' successor, his son Henry, made wooden plate cameras on the premises – a few of them are still around – and started a collection of lantern slides which were hired out all over the region with "oxy-hydrogen limelight apparatus" which often started fires in village halls. There were dozens of Scriptural slides and also a unique collection of views of every major town and city in the country. This collection came to a sad end; after the war the firm offered the slides free to all the places pictured, but only three councils took up the offer. All but the Bristol slides, which went to Mr. Reece Winstone, went on the tip.

Henry Husbands the second handed over to his son Alfred in the 1880s, when the firm was selling gold pince-nez for four guineas and ladies' double-acting spring eye-glasses, folding into a tortoiseshell case, for 15s., as well as glass eyes from 10s. 6d., thermometers, barometers, pedometers, opera and field glasses, electric bells, conversation tubes and ear-trumpets, along with the cameras. Alfred was also interested in radio, and carried out experiments in transmitting from a tent on the Downs. He was, incidentally, the third shop-owner in Bristol to install electricity.

In those days, opticians' businesses were deregulated, for in the regular pamphlets that Alfred published, he mentions that "it is no uncommon thing for a person to go to a stationer, jeweller, chemist, pawnbroker, or even a linen draper, and say 'I want a pair of spectacles please'."

Alfred also made early movies: he filmed the visit of the Prince of Wales to Bristol in 1902, and another photographic treasure which still exists is a set of photographs of the building of the Suspension Bridge in 1862-63, taken by Henry, Jnr.

Alfred died in 1932 and his daughter, the present owner's mother, became a director. In the Blitz, the roof of the shop was twice demolished by bombs and much of the surveying and marine equipment was commandeered by the Admiralty, including a historic binocular microscope which was kept under a glass dome in the shop. After the war, Husbands stopped making instruments and lenses on the premises and in the Sixties dropped the optician's side altogether, in an agreement with Dunscombes. The firm now has nine branches – and possibly more in Australia!

Bristolians who did not want to buy camera equipment and take pictures themselves went instead to a photographic studio to have family portraits taken.

In the 1880s they went to **George Frederick Bromhead's** studio at 1, Regent Street, Clifton, where they would be posed in front of a tasteful fern and a nicely draped curtain, and physically clamped into position for several minutes. On one occasion, Fred Bromhead, as he was always known, clamped a Gloucestershire farmer in position, went upstairs and forgot all about him. When he released his client, the man remarked that he would never have had his picture taken if he had known how painful it would be.

Fred Bromhead was a self-taught photographer who soon embarked on a new branch of the art: commercial photography. On his specially adapted tricycle, with a platform on the back to carry his 10 inch by 12 inch plate camera and tripod, he would pedal around Bristol and even further afield, taking pictures of construction work. He did a set of the

The only surviving portrait of photographer Fred Bromhead was obtained from an Australian branch of the family: all the Bristol photographs were destroyed in the Blitz.

Royal Edward Dock while it was being built, and took early photos of the Bristol Aeroplane Works at Filton. He also took a great many shots of sporting groups, the earliest being a picture of the Flax Bourton Cricket XI in 1884, the date the business started. Much later in life, he reluctantly bought a horseless carriage, but persisted in riding his tricycle right up to his death in 1931.

His son Jack was literally born in the darkroom above the studios, and started off a career in insurance, until his absent-minded father realised he had left school, and told him to hand in his notice, and join the family firm. They moved to Merchants Road, Clifton, in 1905, where the business remained until 1940, when it was bombed, destroying a priceless collection of photos of West Country life. The worst irony of all was that the following morning, Jack Bromhead was due to take pictures of the bombed bank building next door. He had to borrow a camera to take the shot. The firm then moved to its present premises at 157, Whiteladies Road; it had been a small hotel, then a night club for officers, complete with a ballroom, which became the studio. Jack's son Christopher is now the owner and the firm still does studio portraits, but without the clamps. The photograph of Fred Bromhead was one he tracked down in Australia, and owned by a cousin. German bombs had even destroyed the portrait of the founder.

Better than a photograph was an original oil-painting. The place to go a century and a half ago was **Frost and Reed,** in Clare Street. The firm was founded in 1808 by William Hill, whose son sold it to John Frost in 1858; he moved to Clare Street, where he advertised himself as "Carver, Gilder, Print seller, Wholesale and retail artists' colourman and drawing paper depot". At some stage he was appointed carver and gilder to Queen Victoria. He eventually handed over to his nephew Walter, who started selling original paintings as well as prints, and then went into partnership with William Reed in 1875. The firm became art publishers as well, and Frost went as far as the United States to sell the firm's reproductions, which were of sporting, topographical, animal and marine subjects, and mezzotints of works by painters such as Reynolds, Lawrence and Gainsborough.

They also started buying and selling paintings, and in 1908 owned a gallery in London; when it was bombed in 1943 they moved to Bond Street and started dealing in Old Masters, selling very profitably to America. They handled many famous paintings and dealt with some exceptional works by de Hooch, Van Dyke and Constable; the Tate Gallery bought one Constable they had handled. Other works sold to national museums were by Corot, Monet and Sisley, and the firm figured in some exciting auction-room dramas. Clients earlier this century included members of the Royal family, a past president of the United States, newspaper magnates such as Randolph Hearst, and Lawrence of Arabia.

Walter Frost died in 1930, and his daughter Edith became governing director; in 1946 his grandson joined the firm briefly, but there the family connection ended. The carving, gilding and framing side of the business continued, and picture restoration was added, with craftsmen's factories set up in St. George, the firm's present home, in 1946. The Clare Street premises, which were damaged in the Blitz – on one occasion a giant cauldron of valuable cooking fat was found lodged in the roof – continued trading until 1981 when the entire operation was moved to St. George. The firm is now owned by the HTV Group.

Another good investment for Bristolians was jewellery and plate. The earliest jewellers acted as bankers, dealing in bullion and investments, in gold and silver plate, and quite often they made loans, or had a pawnbroking business as well.

Parsons the jewellers, who started as a clockmaking business, have the distinction of being the oldest surviving jewellery firm in the country, dating fom 1710. With solicitors Latcham Montague, founded the same year, these two firms are the oldest in Bristol.

Parsons was founded by George Edgecumbe in Old Market, on a site in Redcross Street. He had trained as a brass founder and from this had developed an interest in clock-making. His son John married an Elizabeth Parsons, and their son George took the business over: Eric Parsons, the present owner, is the seventh generation to run the business – and sadly he is the last of the line.

The first shop was a private house, built in 1720, and the clockmaking and jewellery making was carried out on the ground floor. As the firm prospered, they used the front garden, which had a frontage on Old Market, to build another shop, no. 15, and the family traded there until 1966, when the premises were demolished to make way for the Old Market roundabout.

Eric Parsons, rummaging in the attic of the old Queen Anne house, before it, too, was demolished, found a 17th century French painting, which he presented to the city. Among his prized family heirlooms are a 1770 long case clock and a bracket clock of 1820, made by his ancestors. He now trades in a new shop in Penn Street.

Chillcotts, The Park Street jewellers, certainly ran a pawnbroking business, because the discreet chute, provided for customers who wanted to pledge goods anonymously after hours, can still be seen at the back of the building. Pawnbroking went on until 1965.

The firm was established by Alfred Chillcott in Host Street in 1808, and he was joined by his son William Thomas. In the 1850s they moved to St. Augustine's Parade, where the old Bristol Omnibus offices were until recently, and evidently did well since, a few years later, they bought one of the best houses in Park Street, No.47, which had belonged to Henry Cruger, Bristol's only American Lord Mayor and MP; he must have bought the house soon after it was built. Chillcotts were one of the first to convert a private Park Street house into a shop, though the present frontage, with its elaborate pillars and double-storey entrance hall, were added in 1903. The company also took over the house on the opposite corner of Great George Street to sell antiques and furniture from 1906 until the early Seventies, and ran regular auction sales there.

In the Second World War, the founder's great-grandson Hubert Chillcott, was alone in the shop on the night of the Blitz when much of Park Street was destroyed. Chillcott's was one of the few left standing in that section of the street, and Hubert, being concerned about the valuable jewellery on the premises, gathered it together and escaped through a trap-door into the street. He took his treasure to the nearby graveyard at St. George's Church, and hid it behind a tombstone – it was still there in the morning when he went to recover it.

When Hubert Chillcott died in 1965, the firm became part of the Northern Goldsmiths Group.

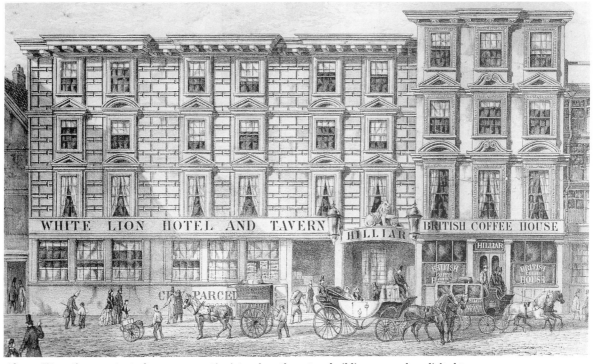

Above: Were there protests from conservationists when these two buildings were demolished to make way for the Grand Hotel? The White Lion was one of Bristol's famous coaching inns.

Below: The W. Kemp shop on the corner of High Street and Corn Street where Cary Grant bought an engagement ring in 1933. Pictured in 1955.

There are two **Kemps** the jewellers in Bristol, W.W. Kemp and Kemp Bros. The founders were brothers who fell out and went their separate ways; fortunately the third and fourth generation of cousins are now on speaking terms.

The first Kemp to set up as a watch and clockmaker was William Wickenden Kemp who in 1881 opened a shop at 60, Stokes Croft, then a posh shopping area. He was a practical clockmaker himself, and quite a few Bristolians still own clocks he made. He was also appointed by Bristol Corporation as Bristol's official clockwinder, and from 1890 to 1920, went around the city winding and regulating all the public and church clocks. He made one of them, the clock still to be seen at Arley Chapel, Cheltenham Road.

From Stokes Croft the business moved to the corner of Corn Street, where, thanks to its proximity to the Grand Hotel, the firm had many famous customers. In fact, staff had to close the shop when, in 1933, word got round to the public that Cary Grant was inside, choosing an engagement ring for his first bride, Virginia Cherrill. Vic Oliver, who often appeared at the Hippodrome, was another regular customer. The shop was moved to Westbury on Trym in 1961.

Kemp Bros. of Union Street, the other branch of the family, started up in 1889, and so just miss the centenary qualification for being included in this chapter.

A centre of social life in Victorian Bristol was the **Grand Hotel.** It was built in 1869 on the site of two very famous inns and staging posts, The White Lion and The White Hart. The new hotel was at first known as the White Lion Hotel, but was renamed in 1874. Foster and Wood were the architects of this Italianate new building which the *Western Daily Press* praised as "the first instance of the introduction of artistic decoration of the higher class in Bristol."

The new hotel had all mod cons: a speaking tube between the manager's office and every head of department, an immense roaster in the kitchen and a hundred hogsheads of ale in stock, not to mention dozens of bottles of vintage wine in its cellar. On opening day, curious citizens of all classes poured in to inspect the new hotel and to drink to its success. The owners were clearly aiming at a popular clientele, for their opening dinner menu was priced at 1s. 6d., and was intended to "furnish a good article at a moderate price, in accordance with the spirit of the age."

One way of making the new enterprise pay was to build shops along the ground floor frontage, where the hotel restaurant is now. Also gone are the white lion symbol of its original name, and a glass canopy which survived until the last war.

The hotel became the place where the famous stayed: actors and actresses, comedians and variety artists playing at the Hippodrome, the Prince's and the Theatre Royal would stay at the Grand. Cary Grant, local boy-made-good, stayed there when he made his first visit back to his home town after making his name in Hollywood. And the hotel played a strange role in the last war, as a stop-over point for British agents, VIP's or exiled royalty who were being flown out of Whitchurch Aerodrome to Lisbon. Amongst those who stopped at the Grand en route were Queen Wilhelmina and Prince Bernhardt of the Netherlands, the Crown Prince of Norway, the Duke of Alba and Mrs Eleanor Roosevelt. One guest bound for Lisbon never arrived. Actor Leslie Howard spent a night at the Grand before taking the plane which was attacked and shot down by enemy fighters over the Bay of Biscay.

The hotel itself was badly damaged during the Blitz, with over 500 doors and windows smashed in one raid alone, when all the gas and electricity was cut off. Winston Churchill came to have a bath there after spending a night in Box Tunnel, and the water had to be heated in milk churns. The elegant ballroom was gutted, and when banqueting began again after the war, a marquee was erected inside its shell.

In 1959 the Grand celebrated its 90th birthday in style, with a three course dinner of mushroom soup, Dover sole and pudding on offer for 9s. 6d.; for their centenary in 1969, everyone wore Victorian dress, including the waiters, and a centenary ale was brewed.

Older by one year is the **St. Vincent Rocks Hotel,** opened in 1868 "opposite the Serpentine Walk", or Zig-Zag. The two houses had merely gone up in the world, for they had been boarding houses almost continuously since they were built in the 1780s, as were most of the now sought-after properties in Sion Row and Sion Hill. These houses were lodgings for visitors to the Hotwell and the resort of Clifton, and remained so up to the end of the 19th century.

In the 1840s, Nos. 1 and 2 belonged to Mr. and Mrs. Charles Minifie. He ran a tailor's business in College Green, while his wife, Sarah, ran the lodging house and the "bath house" next door, where the exit of the Sion Spring was. The bath house, on the corner of West Mall, was built in 1798 and fitted up with great luxury, with several baths and a reading room. It was run by a Thomas Bird, but the 70 degree water did not attract much custom and in 1803 the pump room "calculated for any genteel business" was advertised to let. The Minifies eventually took it over, and let part of it to a bookseller.

The lodgings at Nos. 1 and 2 became even more desirable once the Suspension Bridge was opened in 1864, so it was a substantial business that the Minifies sold to a newly-formed joint-stock company who wanted to turn it into a hotel. Apart from the Zig-Zag Bar, which hides the side elevation of No. 1, the two houses and the bath house still look much the same as they did in 1868.

As well as socialising, a major interest for Victorian men was sport, and in particular, shooting. Between 1782 and 1850, there were some 50 gunsmiths and gun-sellers trading in Bristol, but only one of them has survived, **George Gibbs** of Perry Road. The firm was founded, probably in 1830, by James and George Gibbs, in Redcliff Street, then moved to Thomas Street, Corn Street and Clare Street later in the century.

Many of Bristol's gun firms dealt in the export market to the colonies, and George Gibbs supplied rifles for big game hunting in the 1860s; they were famous for designing the Farquaharson Metford .505 big game rifle which was exported all over the world, even as far as Russia and Japan, as well as Africa and India. This enormously successful rifle elicited the following testimonial, one to make today's conservationists blench.

"On the 5th of this month while on safari, I was called at 5.30 a.m. as a native informed me that elephant were raiding his intame garden, so I rushed out, picked up the .505, and in half an hour came to a herd of seven elephants in the long grass just clear of the village. I got up to within 12 yards of them and dropped two, the rest made off and I followed, and owing to there being natives around, did not go far, and in a few minutes I came up to them again and dropped four more; only one was left and he returned to the first two, and I shot him at 6–7 yards. I think this is the finest christening any rifle ever had. Seven elephant before break-fast!"

Above: Veals Tower Hill gunsmith's shop, demolished in the 'fifties road-building programme. Pictured circa 1930.

Below: The Veals brothers shared the popular passion for bicycling, in the early 1900s.

This heartless account was written in Kenya in the 1920s.

Not surprisingly, George Gibbs, son of the founder, was a crack shot who represented England and who once scored 57 consecutive bullseyes in front of King Edward VII in 1909.

His father and uncle had both joined the Bristol Rifle Volunteers when they were re-formed in 1859 (Bristol's 1798 Volunteers were the first in the country), and a craze for rifle drill and shooting-ranges resulted; when the Drill Hall was built at the top of Park Street in 1861, there were 1,000 members in 10 companies, and the firm of George Gibbs had the contract to supply them, since he was an expert designer and manufacturer of guns and maker of ammunition.

His son George became Colonel of one of the Volunteer Corps, and he would, as a birthday treat, let his little daughter head the parade on a big horse. The Colonel, a keen sportsman, started the Clifton Beagles, and was a friend of W.G. Grace. He once became the talk of the town for shooting down an effigy of a parliamentary candidate, hung by pranksters from the Suspension Bridge.

Another gunsmith in the city was **Samuel Veals,** who began his gun-making and gunsmith's business in Tower Hill in 1846. The family stayed there for 130 years, until the business moved, because of redevelopment, to its present home in Old Market.

The early business was a cutler's as well, and in the basement of the Tower Hill shop (where once, during a building project, a stone tomb, a Bristol farthing and an 18th century sundial were found) there was knife-grinding and sharpening equipment. When the Victorian owners of the new villas in Redland and Cotham needed their spacious lawns cared for, they bought lawn-mowers, and then took them to Veals to be repaired and sharpened; thus a new kind of business grew up. Until the Second World War, Veals sold guns and lawn-mowers and repaired both, as well as sharpening scissors and cut-throat razors. But when a member of the fourth generation of the family, Sev Veals, came back from the war, he announced that he never wanted to see another gun in his life, and his father's friend, MP Ernie Bevin suggested that Veals should start stocking fishing-tackle instead. They started with a few cartons and from this grew into the largest fishing-tackle firm in the region. The lawn-mower side of the business went to Easton, but closed in 1970, and the guns disappeared after the last war. Five generations of the Veals family have now worked in the firm.

7 – The Printed word

"I never knew a city so mercantile that was so literary," said Bristol's Poet Laureate Robert Southey in 1813. This was true enough after 1700. Before then, the majority of Bristolians were illiterate, and this is reflected in the lack of printers and booksellers in the city, though the first recorded bookseller is Eliazer Edgar, who petitioned to become a freeman in 1620.

The first press in Bristol was a King Charles I portable press, set up in 1643, and the first Bristol publisher was John Cary, who, in 1695, published an *Essay on the State of England.* His printer was William Bonney, who brought out the first provincial weekly newspaper in the country, the *Bristol Post Boy,* from 1702 to 1712. On his death the business split into two concerns, *Felix Farley's Bristol Journal* and *Sarah Farley's Bristol Journal,* both single sheets folded into four and containing mostly London news and Bristol advertisements. The papers were distributed on horseback to a very wide area – as far as Devon and Cornwall, North and South Wales, London and Liverpool in the 1790s.

The city continued to have a variety of weekly papers: besides the two *Journals* there was the *Bristol Mercury,* the *Bristol Times,* the *Advertiser* and the *Clifton Chronicle,* and all of them were still going when Bristol's first penny morning newspaper, the **Western Daily Press,** was established in 1858, as one of the first provincial dailies in the country.

The *Western Daily Press* was started by a Scot, Peter Stewart Macliver and a Bristolian, Walter Reid, on a hand-fed press at 1, Broad Street. The output was 1,500 to 2,000 papers an hour, and in the first editorial the Editor said that his great mission was "to elevate, to guide, to instruct, to interest the people, and render the mass of mankind more and more faithful to the trust they hold for themselves and their communities." The paper had advertisements on its front page for Unfailing Cures for Corns, Professor Camp's Walnut Pomade, brass cornice poles, Cotterell's Steamed Printed and Parisian wallpapers, Men's Summer Suits at 12s. and Maggs' iron bedsteads.

The *WDP* cost one penny and the weekly delivery charge was 6d. In 1865 it bought up the *Times and Mirror;* in 1869 started the *Bristol Observer,* a weekly, and in 1877, Bristol's first evening paper, the *Bristol Evening News.* In 1886 the *WDP* moved to a grand new building in Baldwin Street; the bricks had been specially made and the lino-type machines were installed on the top floor, which had a glass roof; there was a speaking-tube system, with whistles, throughout the whole building.

Newspaper competition was always fierce; up to the newspaper war of the Thirties, Bristol had six daily papers. The WDP was taken over by Bristol Limited Press in 1960.

The citizens seem to have been avid readers of books, too, from the 18th century on, when rates of literacy were improving. From then onwards, the city had a healthy number of booksellers and the first circulating library, with 200 volumes, was established in Wine Street in 1728.

In Victorian times, the number of booksellers and lending libraries was astonishing: *Hunt's Guide to Bristol, 1850,* lists 62 booksellers. Since the 18th century there had been many circulating libraries, the most famous of which had been run in Hotwells by

The Western Daily Press celebrates Queen Victoria's Jubilee in 1897.

the milkwoman poetess Ann Yearsley. There were also four reading rooms at that period, and a music lending library. In the 1880s, Massingham's lending library boasted 50,000 volumes at their Regent Street, Clifton, premises. Possibly the middle classes thought municipal libraries were beneath them. But the public library tradition was strong in the city, beginning with the library of the Calendars, a trade guild who lent out their precious books to selected citizens in the 15th century. Bristol also had the second public library in the country, after Norwich, when in 1613, Robert Redwood gave to the city a lodge near his house in the Marsh (Queen's Square) for a library; this was the nucleus of the King Street Library, built in 1740. Bristol also had an active Library Society founded in 1772, and the first branch public library opened in St. Philips in 1876; to be followed by eight more by the end of the century.

The pious Victorians were also great buyers of religious literature and Bristol had an **SPCK** depot as early as 1810, in Corn Street; it was puzzlingly described as "open every day *except Sunday*". The depot, which later became a shop, run by local supporters, sold tracts, prayer books and the Society's bibles. Another source of improving literature was the **Evangelical and Christian Literature Bible Warehouse** set up by George Muller, soon after his conversion in 1843 and before he opened his first orphanage. He founded his Scriptural Knowledge Institution in the same year, and one of its objects was to "circulate the Holy Scripture and to supply the wants of missionaries."

The SKI started at 3, Wilson Street, and moved in 1852 to Park Street, where the work was carried on for 90 years until the shop was destroyed in the Blitz; a new shop near the original site opened in 1957. Profits from the sale of books still go to missionaries and provide bibles in countries where they are in short supply, as in Muller's time, when the SKI supported six day-schools, two Sunday schools and one adult school. The advertisements used to promise "bibles available every day."

Of the large number of secular booksellers of the 18th and 19th centuries, only the name of **George's** of Park Street survives. William George was born in Dunster in 1830, and he was sent to Bristol at the age of 12 to learn the business of bookselling from his uncle, William Strong, who had a shop in Clare Street. Strong had had all his stock burned in the Bristol Riots, so his nephew did not take over the business but started up on his own in 1847, at 15, Bath Street, at the tender age of 17, with a capital of £50. He paid 3s. 6d. a week rent.

By 1848 he had issued his first catalogue; in 1850 he moved to 29, Bath Street, and his capital three years later stood at £1,000. He moved to the fashionable Park Street in 1871, and by 1878 his stock was valued at £4,000. He was aware of the American market, too, for in 1876 he prepared a catalogue for circulation in the USA.

His sons, Charles and Frank, both showed an aptitude for bookselling and became partners in 1884 when the firm became William George and Sons. This gave William more time to pursue his special interests, topography and genealogy. He was largely responsible for galvanising local opinion in favour of building the Cabot Tower, and for the tardy recognition by the city of its most controversial son, Thomas Chatterton. Frank played a leading role in the foundation of a public library at Weston-super-Mare.

William George died in 1900 and his son Frank in 1905, and the remaining son,

Above: Old technology! The Western Daily Press linotype room in the old offices in Baldwin Street were the most modern in the country, in 1858.

Below: The ancestor of today's Western Daily Press. This sign can still be seen over the doorway of their former offices in St Stephen's Street.

Charles, carried on through the Great War with the help of his daughter; but his failing health made him sell out in 1928 to Blackwells of Oxford, where until 1908 there had been a branch of George's. From 1928 the family connection ceased. George's were one of the few Park Street firms to come through the Blitz unscathed: they lost only three books, damaged by flying glass.

Printing became a major Bristol trade from the second half of the 18th century, but these were mostly small jobbing firms which were short-lived. With the first machine-presses, larger concerns were born. **John Wright and Company** claim to be the first to have installed machine presses, in the 1830s, and they went on to become big printers of street and trade directories and time-tables, and in the 1880s began to specialise in medical textbooks.

Most printers had to content themselves with small everyday jobs. An idea of a printer's life in the first half of the 19th century is provided by the story of **Thomas Ozora Elworthy,** born in 1845, and by the age of nine working for a printer as an errand boy, six days a week, from 7 a.m. to 8 p.m., for 2s. a week. He learned all branches of the trade and opened his own business in 1868, at the age of only 23, in a side street near the almshouses in Old Market.

He carried on an 18th century tradition, too, by opening a British Workmen's Coffee Tavern, where meetings and club activities were organised. Needless to say, he was a keen supporter of temperance and used to do mission work at the Bethel Ship, berthed by the Hotwell Road.

Thomas Ozora Elworthy went in for bread–and–butter printing of church magazines, concert tickets, programmes, auctioneers' posters and so on. Three of his four sons went into the business and the oldest, Francis Ozora, became managing director, only to outlive the death of his father, aged 92, by two years. The firm then moved to a small factory in Tower Lane, but had to move again, because Fry's wanted the site, at the back of the Grand Hotel.

Francis Ozora's son had not followed in the family tradition, and this, plus the outbreak of the Second World War, caused problems, until his grandson Hubert Francis changed career and took over in 1946. The firm had to move again in 1948 to Broad Street and again in 1953 to Host Street, where in 1967, the fourth generation, Christopher Martin, joined the company.

The multiplicity of jobs that a Victorian printer could expect to do is well illustrated by the work of **Allen Davies and Company,** founded in 1886 by a pair of Methodists, Edward Allen, a stationer, and Henry Davies, a compositor. They started trading in Nelson Street in a house on three floors, printing butchers' meat tickets, advertisements, and catalogues like the one for the great Industrial and Fine Art Exhibition of 1893, and producing beautifully bound account books and ledgers. The business grew and by 1892 they had taken over a block in Rupert Street known as the Old Sugar House.

As with so many firms, one company's special needs were met by another; the expanding boot and shoe industry in Kingswood meant that cardboard boxes were needed, so Allen Davies started supplying them from 1893, delivering them in covered

The little acorn that was George's Park Street bookshop, seen here in 1947, before the firm expanded further down the street.

One of the most famous comic novels ever written was published by Arrowsmiths: an illustration from J.K. Jerome's Three Men in a Boat.

horse–drawn wagons. After the First World War came modernisation: a Heath Robinson arrangement of pulleys and belts for the gas driven machinery was replaced by electricity, and new packaging and wrapping systems were developed. One early shrink –wrap system, Kolatarap and Kolataform, which automatically wrapped cartons of jars and cans, also sealed the firm's fortunes, and the process was eventually patented world –wide; the success was so huge that Metal Box acquired the licence. Another Allen Davies invention was the famous Fixecure card which hangs in pubs and shops, selling snacks from a card with a series of packets attached. This Seventies patent revolutionised the sale of snacks, so that nowadays the firm has a turnover of £3 million a year and sells to Europe, Saudi Arabia and the Yemen.

Just before the last war, the firm moved to a site in St. James Barton, where, in the Blitz, but for resourceful firewatchers, all would have gone up in the flames from a nearby building. The firewatchers nailed lithoplates over the windows. After the war, the firm snapped up anything saleable, including 25,000 toilet rolls and the first biros, which sold for £5 each.

Few people know that it was a Bristol printer and publisher who launched two great comic novels into the world. **Arrowsmith's** brought out *Three Men in a Boat* in 1889 and *Diary of a Nobody* in 1892, to say nothing of books by Conan Doyle and Anthony Hope. In the 1880s it was Arrowsmith's who published the early "shilling shockers" sold on railway bookstalls.

The firm was started in 1854 by Isaac Arrowsmith whose first venture as a printer was a *Penny Timetable of Steam Packets and Railway Trains.*

Arrowsmith moved to Quay Street in 1857, and there the firm stayed for 97 years, printing for such diverse clients as Bristol University and the railways. They also printed hymns and cricket scorecards, including the famous one featuring the match between Bristol and England in 1863. They published W.G. Grace's book and still have several querulous letters from the great man to prove it, as well as a much cherished letter from Florence Nightingale, whose article they were printing for a learned journal. They were great printers and publishers of Bristoliana, and have printed every issue of *The Cliftonian* since 1870.

As publishers they ought to have made money from their best-sellers, but *Three Men in a Boat* was pirated in America, and sales of *Diary of a Nobody* were small at first. In fact their best success came with a now forgotten best-seller by Hugh Conway (the pseudonym for Bristol auctioneer Fred Fargus) titled *Called Back,* a book which Arrowsmith bought for £80 in 1883.

There was a long association with the railways: in 1869, Arrowsmith's printed for the Bristol and Exeter Railway the *General Regulations,* with illustrations of frock-coated and top-hatted operators of signal flags, and they also printed railway excursion posters and pamphlets advertising extra trains for GWR and then British Rail.

In 1974, at their present home in Winterstoke Road, the firm moved into the world of new technology and programmed mathematical setting and started specialising in educational and scientific journals. Right up to 1962, they had their annual outing or waysgooze; the first was in 1856 when "Mr. Arrowsmith led out the men in his employ to enjoy a rustic holiday. At 8 a.m. they assembled round his breakfast table in Berkeley Place, which was bountifully and tastefully covered... The great day ended when at 11 p.m. the omnibus was loaded with the company, 12 in number, and thence rolling onto towards Clifton, the night was rendered harmonious by the hearty songs of John Bull."

W.H. Smith was one firm which handled Arrowsmith's shilling shockers. This is another firm owing much to Brunel, for bookstalls at railway stations formed a large part of their early business. They opened at Temple Meads in 1865 and at the Bristol and Exeter terminus in 1884, and both stalls remained there until 1905. They did good business: combined receipts for 1893-4 were £5,979, of which £3,332 was accounted for by sales of newspapers, £2,144 from books, £114 from lending-library subscriptions and the rest from miscellaneous business. W.H. Smith were also advertising contractors to the Bristol and Exeter Railway and the GWR, and later to the Portishead Pier and Port Railway Company and the Clifton Down and Avonmouth line. Some of these contracts date back to 1859.

The first Bristol shop was opened in 1905 at 24, Regent Street, Clifton, to supply customers previously served at the railway bookstalls; the profit for the first seven months was just over £80 – and the manager was earning £100 a year plus 20 per cent of the profits. The wholesale side was begun in 1903 with the purchase of a firm in Victoria Street and Thomas Street, and transferred to the present site in Temple Gate in 1937. W.H. Smith also ran a lending library at Whiteladies Gate, around the turn of the century.

While some printing businesses have changed out of all recognition, others are doing virtually the same job they did a century ago. **Alfred Harris,** the bookbinders of Portland Square, are still making, with a little more help from machinery, the same kind of bound ledgers and account books that Joseph Harris made when he started up in 1860, at Broad Street, where he styled himself bookbinder, stationer, machine ruler and account book manufacturer. He supplied law firms and the courts, as now, and was a bookbinder to the printing trade, binding by hand, and later, on heavy sewing machines, anything that needed stitching and covering. Joseph Harris was succeeded by his son Alfred, who in 1929 took on as apprentice Christopher Stacey, the present about-to-retire owner. Alfred went into voluntary liquidation in 1931 for the now ludicrously small sum of £100, and Mr. Stacey bought him out. "Everything was done by hand then," he recalls, "and we mixed all our own glue, and did the rules in the ledgers using a wooden board marked out with brass pins which we had to make ourselves." Little information about the Harris family is available because the Broad Street premises were bombed and all records were lost.

Another different kind of printing was done by **Prestridge,** the rubber-stamp manufacturers now in Southmead.

When College Green was re-designed in 1951, and the statue of Queen Victoria moved, in the foundations were found a bottle containing coins, a copy of the *Western Daily Press* of 1888, and a smashed ceramic plaque.

Prestridge's knew exactly what was on that plaque, because they had made the die for it. It recorded the details of the ceremony when the foundation for the statue was laid in 1888.

The firm was founded in 1870 by two American brothers. They came over from the

States with a brand new process; the art of making india rubber blocks for date stamps, advertising material, and dies for marking pottery and china. One of the brothers must have had Bristol family links, for his name was Edward Colston Prestridge. They set up in a basement in Small Street and enjoyed a complete monopoly; they were the first firm of their kind in the country and were soon supplying offices and shops and industries far and wide. One of their earliest customers was and is Wills.

They made their rubber stamps on a handpress, which survives, and which was still in use until a few years ago: metal type was set up, a plaster mould was taken and filled with rubber. One of their specialities, rarely called for today, was making dies to stamp into drink manufacturers' pottery jars, demi-johns and barrels, work which they did for breweries, ginger-beer makers and grocery firms like Keillers, who still use Prestridge dies for the Dundee marmalade pots. The now defunct Pountney Pottery was a big customer.

What became of the Prestridge brothers is not known, but in the early Thirties they sold out to Henry Garland, who moved the firm to what is now the Foster's Rooms. He bought the business to set up his sons Frank and Jack, and his grandson John is now in charge. During the Second World War, the firm made thousands of dies for marking ammunition cases, and since bureaucracy was plentiful during a war, they thrived.

Two other important printing developments took place in the city, the earlier being the 1798 publication by Joseph Cottle, bookseller in High Street, of Wordsworth's and Coleridge's Lyrical Ballads, thus helping to launch the Romantic movement in poetry.

In 1925, sculptor and artist Eric Gill first tried out his new type-face, when he designed the fascia of Cleverdon's bookshop in Charlotte Street, thus christening the famous Gill-Sans; another first was the invention by William Friese-Green in 1898, of a filmsetting device that would produce letters for printing – a forerunner of photo-setting.

Another Bristol printer left an architectural treasure behind him: Edward Everard the printer, who set up in Broad Street in 1901, was strongly influenced by the Arts and Crafts movement, and built on his works a magnificent tiled facade in Art Nouveau style, a monument to the art of printing in Bristol, right down to a spelling mistake!

8 – The Professionals.

Bristol's flourishing trade from the 17th century onwards brought much business to the newly established professions of the law, accountancy and surveying, and once again the city can claim some firsts.

The longest surviving legal practice in the country was started in Bristol in 1710; of the seven accountancy firms considered to be the earliest in Britain, three were founded in Bristol, and the city can also claim the oldest surveying practice in the land.

In 1710, Bristol attorney Thomas Latcham witnessed a document which attested that a certain Thomas Simmonds and his wife Sarah were inhabitants of the parish of Filton, in order that they should qualify for charitable relief.

This framed document hangs on the wall in the offices of **Latchams Montague and Niblett,** solicitors, of Stokes Croft, for a very good reason: it is proof that Latchams is the oldest law firm in the country, and it is quite possible that Thomas Latcham was practicing even earlier. The business was handed down from father to son until it reached Charles Latcham, who was born in 1811. He had no son, but his sister Maria married a Charles Montague, and the Montagues inherited the firm until the 1920s when a Montague daughter married Geoffrey Niblett. In Victorian Bristol, the Montagues were Clerks to the Justices at Chipping Sodbury, and in this century, to the Justices of Staple Hill. The firm has been Clerk to the Commoners of Durdham Down for over a century – a job which entails over-seeing the grazing of sheep!

Another proof of Bristol's pre-eminence as a legal city is the fact that **Bristol Law Society**, founded in 1770, is the oldest in England, and senior to the Law Society itself, which was set up in 1825. Until Bristol had a Law Society, attorneys did not neccessarily have to read Law at Oxford or Cambridge, or even have to pass an exam. They were appointed by the Lord Chancellor, on character references alone. The actual title of attorney was abolished in England in 1873, because by that time the word had become synonymous with a knave or swindler!

Definitely neither knave or swindler was Jeremiah Osborne, whose name survives in the firm of **Osborne Clarke,** now with offices in Queen Charlotte Street. Jeremiah was evidently working as a solicitor in 1745, for then, according to Latimer, he petitioned the Corporation over the disqualification of his father Joseph, a shipwright, as a freeman of the city. Osborne senior was living in a house near the Limekilns in Hotwells, that was all but 18 inches over the then county border of Somerset. Jeremiah won his case.

The firm must have been well-known, for Jeremiah's son Robert acted for Brunel, accompanying the engineer on surveys on land between Reading and Bath for the Great West Railway. Robert negotiated with the local landowners and kept an eye on costings. He also advised Brunel when he was considering his entry for the Suspension Bridge competition, and according to a letter, tried to discourage him from trying.

The other partner in the firm was William Clarke who started up in 1770 when he joined William and Edward Parker at their practice, which dated from 1725, at Broad Street. He became sole partner in 1799 and was the first of six generations of Clarkes in the legal profession, the sixth being Charles Clarke who is still practising. The most famous of the family was William Lawton Clarke, who was Lord Mayor in 1843; he was an alcoholic with a wooden leg, and caused consternation by travelling in the Lord Mayor's coach with his wooden leg hanging out of the window. In 1819, he had a case to plead in Chancery in London; he took the stage coach and was snowed up in Calne for ten days. When he finally arrived, he found the case had been heard in his absence – and that he had won it.

One of the founders of Bristol Law Society in 1770 was Daniel Burges, who came to the city from Wiltshire and eventually became Bristol Clerk of Arraigns, a post he held until 1791; his son Daniel II became Town Clerk, and was caught up in the Bristol Riots. Daniel Burges III also held the same post.

But it was Daniel II's second son, Edward, who actually set up the present practice, now known as **Burges Salmon;** he qualified in 1837 and one of his first professional concerns during his articles at the Council House had involved the litigation that resulted from the damage caused during the Bristol riots.

In 1840 he became Clerk to the Committee appointed by Bristol Corporation to carry out the Bristol Improvement Act, which concerned road improvements and traffic management, and even covered regulation of hanging balconies, posting of street names and controlling "the use of profane language to the annoyance of the inhabitants, or the pulling or ringing of doorbells without lawful excuse".

He became a large property owner and his expertise led naturally to a practice which at that time concentrated on the purchase and sale of property, and he became a recognised authority on property values in the city.

Edward Burges's son, Col. W.E. Parry Burges (a land agent as well as solicitor), continued the practice on his father's death in 1890 and began a military tradition which persisted. He was a Colonel in the Glosters, like his cousin – Victoria Cross winner, Daniel Travers Burges.

The firm continued to prosper and expand – it now has 16 partners with a staff of well over 100. It has been known by its present name of Burges Salmon since 1947. It was only in the previous year that Edward Burges's old managing clerk, Edwin Light Wyatt, had died aged 97. He joined the firm in 1865 and was still actively employed by them as senior cashier (having mastered the new system of PAYE) at the time of his death, with an unbroken service of over 80 years. A few months before his death he was sent a personal message from King George VI, congratulating him on his remarkable record.

Most of the old legal firms chopped and changed partners and names over the years, making them very hard to trace, but **Bevan Hancock**, now Bevan Ashford, retained its original name until just recently. The Bevan half started with William Bevan who appears in Bristol Law Lists for 1815: he had as his first partner Meshack Brittan, the man who sorted out the years of mismanagement and chicanery involved in the Corporation's handling of the many charitable trusts in the city; he found scandals galore and organised swift retribution.

Charles Bevan joined the firm and worked with his father until 1850, when it seems they quarrelled, and the son set up on his own. William Bevan then took on as partner Charles Hancock, son of a clergyman who had been head of the Cathedral School. Charles Hancock had weak health; he was bald at the age of 27, and an extraordinary .

shape, long in the body and short in the legs, and he used to interview clients sitting on a chair with his feet on the edge of the seat, which disconcerted them more than somewhat. He became a city councillor and was famous for his plain speech; when his partner's widow, Mrs. Charles Bevan, came to see him about a lost carpet, he asked her, since she was a large lady, whether she had it concealed about her person. He turned down the chance to be Lord Mayor on the pretext that he preferred his own carriage to the Mayoral coach, which was soft-sprung and would therefore make him sea-sick.

Charles Hancock also figured in the brewery wars in 1878, when Georges, the major brewery in Bristol, put its shares on the market. The other small brewing firms combined to form Bristol United Breweries, and in 1890 Charles Hancock became a director, a connection which carried on until 1952, when Georges finally bought up Bristol United Breweries; this valuable client became the foundation of extensive licensing business which still goes on.

The old premises at 24, Baldwin Street were like Dodson and Fogg's in *Pickwick Papers,* with one telephone and speaking-tubes, which proved handy when a bankrupt came in and announced he was going to shoot three people – his creditor, his lawyer and himself. The lawyer in question, G.H. Boucher, said he would telephone to get the other victim in, and left the room, snatching the revolver as he left. The office boys were then able to dash in and overpower the maddened bankrupt with their ebony rulers. The offices were moved to 25, Baldwin Street in 1927, and have been there ever since.

Charles Bevan had no children, but Charles Hancock had a son, Robert, who joined the firm in 1890; he stayed only four years – maybe he found his eccentric father too much to cope with – and left to become a manager of a tea-station in Ceylon. The last descendant of the Hancock family, Ray Boucher, a grandson, left in 1956.

One of the strangest items in the archives of **Cartwrights,** the Marsh Street solicitors, is a 115-year-old wig. It was worn first in 1871 by Thomas Danger, who founded the firm in 1836 in Corn Street. He was appointed Clerk of the Peace for Bristol, and the wig went with the job. The office was held by subsequent partners of the firm until 1971 when the title was abolished and the same wig was passed on from generation to generation.

Frederick Cartwright married Thomas Danger's daughter Katherine, and the new son-in-law became a partner; he was for a time solicitor to Bristol and West Building Society. The last Cartwright died in 1946, but despite various amalgamations with other Bristol firms, the name has survived.

The firm of **Stanley Wasbrough** was founded by William Wasbrough, son of a Bristol brass founder who was an early exploiter of steam power: in 1779 he was granted a patent relating to "Steam Engines for converting a reciprocal motion into a rotary motion." But his son went in for the law, and in 1819 was practising in All Saints' Lane. William married twice, and his second son, Henry Sidney Wasbrough, became a partner in 1842. The Stanley of the title was the husband of one of William's daughters, John Bligh Stanley, who joined the firm in 1830.

H.S. Wasbrough became the Coroner of Bristol in 1868 and held the inaugural meeting for establishing Clifton College, in his Clifton home. Around 1870, he took on a new junior clerk, a certain George White who later became the founder of the Bristol Aeroplane Company. Wasbrough tried to persuade him to qualify as a solicitor, but White moved on to become Secretary of the newly formed Bristol Tramways and Carriage Company: it is pleasing to record that Wasbroughs acted for Sir George for the rest of his life, until 1916.

Henry Wasbrough died in 1892, and his son Charles, who had become a partner in 1875, died nine years later; neither he nor John Stanley had sons, so the family connection died out, though the name has been retained to this day.

Associated with the growing number of legal firms in the city was the establishment of legal stationers' firms. **William Ross** started his business in the heart of legal Bristol in John Street in 1826, producing documents for the legal profession. The documents were copied, in copperplate, on skin, and required great skill; occasionally the firm was called on to produce an illuminated address. They did contracts, deeds, affidavits and wills, but strangely for a firm which existed to make records, few of their own survive.

William Ross II formed a partnership with his nephew Alfred, in 1884, thus establishing the present title, W. and A. Ross. The deed of partnership was a bit one-sided: it said that Alfred was "to devote his whole time to the business; William Lewis Ross only such time as he thinks necessary." Alfred got 30 shillings a week and a share of the profits, determined by his uncle, who plainly got the best of the bargain, since Alfred paid £700 for his partnership.

Four years later, Uncle William died, and Alfred inherited the firm, which was still in the era of the quill pen. Alfred employed law writers to work for him part-time, and would sometimes have to call on them to work through the night on some urgent document which was needed the next day.

Alfred had taken one of his sons, another Alfred, into the firm, but he was killed in the First World War, so when Alfred died in the 1920s, Hubert Ross took over, while his other brother, one of Bristol's earliest motorists, decided to go into the motor trade. The Second World War brought problems: Hubert was called up and, two or three years later, the firm closed down. It was re-started in 1945, with a move to offices in Tailor's Court, in the building which has one of the most famous doorways in Bristol, a beautiful shell hood decorated with the coat of arms of the Guild of Merchant Tailors.

In 1948, the present owner, Ivan Ross, Hubert's son, joined, and gradually the business was transformed. The demand for handwritten copies of documents had declined, thanks to the typewriter, and the emphasis shifted to legal stationery, and later, general stationery, and in 1962 they moved to their present home in Fairfax Street.

The profession of accountancy began with "accomptants", men who managed financial affairs for merchants or landowners. But accountants as we know them first appeared in the late 18th century, and of the seven firms regarded as the founders of the modern profession, three started up in Bristol.

The oldest was begun by Josiah Wade in Queen Square in 1797, in offices which were burned down in the Bristol Riots. This firm eventually became **Tribe Clark,** now owned by Deloitte Haskins and Sells. The work of the earliest firms was mainly in bankruptcy, but after the 1820s they began to grow with the Industrial Revolution, serving the new industries which sprang up.

The next oldest firm, **Curtis Jenkins and Cornwell,** now part of Coopers and Lybrand, was founded in 1816 by Robert Fletcher, with various offices in the Small Street area (a lucky choice, because it meant their archives survived the Riots). In 1839 he took on his son-in-law William Jenkins and a member of his staff, John Curtis, as partners. Fletcher did work for Brunel with regard to the Bristol and Gloucester Railway, and the Bristol and Exeter Railway negotiations with GWR; in 1836 he became accountant to the Clifton Suspension Bridge Trust, a client to this day. Other early clients were Wills and another old tobacco firm, Franklins, and there were others in shipping, glass, distilling and quarrying. Members of Fletcher's staff attended the launching of the s.s. *Great Britain* and the firm has the distinction of being the only one ever to have had a report published by Bristol Corporation, in 1839, when there was a notorious battle between the Corporation and the governors of Queen Elizabeth's Hospital.

The third early firm was **Grace, Darbyshire and Todd,** still in business but now part of KMG Thomson McLintock. In 1818, John Moxham, a Quaker, set up his practice at 5, Exchange Buildings, and in 1861 merged with James Grace and Son, when he took on their name and moved to Corn Street. The firm remained Grace and Son for three generations, until 1919 when partners Darbyshire and Todd joined. They merged with C.J. Ryland and Co. in 1969, and later with Thompson McLintock, now Bristol's biggest accountancy firm.

The firm with what must be one of the most interesting offices in the city is **J. and A.W. Sully,** who work in the Abbey Gatehouse, next door to the Cathedral. Clients have to climb up a series of medieval staircases only four feet wide.

The firm dates back to the 1860s, when James Wood Sully, member of an old Bridgwater family, entered into a partnership in a Sheffield practice. He moved to London in 1877 with his nephew Alfred Willie Sully, and they opened a branch in Corn Street, Bristol, in 1883. The branch did not last long, but Sully's took on several Bristol clients who remain so to this day.

A branch was opened in Bridgwater in 1896 and another in Weston-super-Mare in 1907, and the firm came back to Bristol again in 1917. Their offices were in Corn Street and then Orchard Street in the Second World War, and here the connection with the Cathedral began. Sully's took over the business of Charles Bartlett who was Clerk to the Chapter of Bristol Cathedral. Since then, partners in the business have held this office to this day, and it was this connection which enabled the firm to move into the Gatehouse, formerly the private home of a Canon of the Cathedral, in 1951. There is no longer a Sully working in the firm – the last of them died in 1960.

Another firm which acted as accountants to several of the other old firms in this book is **Solomon Hare,** of Union Street; it was established by Solomon Hare in 1869, and he was accountant to the early tramways firms, taking on the Bristol Tramways in 1869, as well as the Gloucester Tramways Company and the London United Tramway, and in 1898 the firm was elected one of the auditors to the City of Bristol. Another claim to

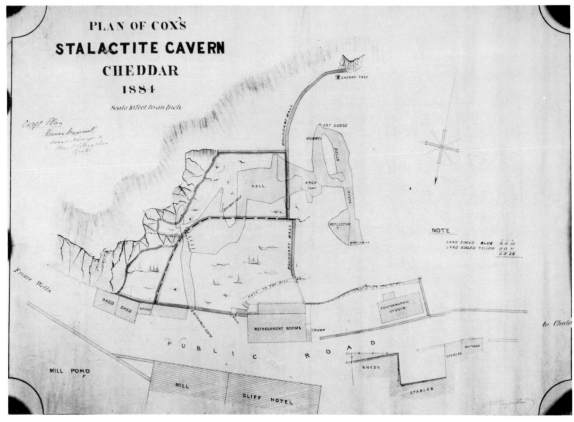

Above: Cox's Stalactite Cavern, Cheddar, as surveyed by J.P. Sturge & Sons in 1884.

Below: Members of the Bristol Stock Exchange 1897. Benjamin Spry Stock was President from 1871—1895.

fame for Solomon Hare was his leadership of the movement to abolish the poll tax in Hotwells.

Benjamin Spry Stock was the first managing director of Bristol and West Building Society, which he helped to found in 1850. He had started his stock broking firm in Small Street in 1844. The firm merged with Beech's of Birmingham in 1979. Tim Stock, descendant of the founder, was chairman until 1987.

Stock Beech are now the largest stock broking firm based in the West Country, and one of the oldest in the country. Following the Stock Exchange's 'Big Bang' in the autumn of 1986, they became the only West Country firm to 'make markets' in shares, specialising in West Country equities and advertising and media. Also in 1986, the firm became incorporated, with The British and Commonwealth Group plc acquiring 55 per cent of the equity.

The firm has played a leading part in privatisations such as British Telecom and British Gas, acting as regional co-ordinator for the share issues.

There is still a co-lateral descendant of the founder of **J.P. Sturge,** the country's oldest surveying firm, working in the business at Berkeley Square. John Young is the great-great-great-great-nephew of Jacob B. Sturge, the Quaker who joined his farmer uncle John Player in his surveying business in 1772. Player and Sturge ran their business from Red House Farm, Coombe Dingle, and Jacob, who was said to be "plain in appearance and manner, industrious and unassuming" and "very peevish", drew fine tithe maps and plans. He trained his son, Young Sturge (Young was his mother's maiden name) as a surveyor, and he set up an office in Small Street in 1799. Young Sturge lived at home and rode into Bristol daily, paying his parents £15 a year for his keep, and 4s. for his horse, while his father provided all the necessary items such as measuring chains, quadrant, spirit level and telescope.

It was a good time to be in this business, during a building boom, and soon to come were the Inclosure Acts and the Tithe Commutation Act which released land for building, which meant that parish maps had to be redrawn by a professional surveyor. Young Sturge did well and in 1810 took on his younger brother, John Player Sturge, at a new office in St. James Barton. Both brothers were known as somewhat dour Quakers and teetotallers; the story goes that when an alderman toasted him, Young replied: "Friend, I hope that in drinking my health thou wilt have a care not to injure thine own." He became Land Steward to Bristol Corporation, a post which passed to his brother and then his nephew.

According to a poem written by one of Young Sturge's daughters, the wives of surveyors had a difficult time. *A Voice of Warning,* written in 1840, lists the miseries: "Perhaps at four the dinner he may fix, but think it well if he arrive by six; hour after hour you look and patient wait, and still no husband enters at the gate."

The coming of the railways to the West Country meant more business for the firm, which by 1838 had acquired land at Temple Meads for the GWR. Young Sturge's nephew William had an even greater connection with the railways: he bought land for several companies and was a noted expert in railway land matters, and a famous witness in legal battles over land wanted by the railway companies.

William's brothers Walter and Robert took care of the land agency business while

William saw to the railway business; he later became surveyor to Bristol Waterworks Company and Bristol Tramways Company, and was responsible for the rating assessment of Somerset. When the Victorian building explosion began, the firm became responsible for the surveying and planning of the new suburbs of Redland, Tyndall's Park, Horfield, and Leigh Woods. William died in 1905, father of a huge family which included daughters who were involved in the women's education movement, and who were among the first students at Bristol University College.

William also left a valuable legacy. During the Second World War his descendants found that he had done all his drawings for Bristol Tramways on fine quality linen, which in a time of clothing coupons, was ideal for making sheets, table-cloths and even shirts. The firm also did practical wartime deeds like introducing to each other two clients, Bristol Waterworks and the manor house at Abbot's Leigh; the latter agreed to supply B.W.'s canteen with rabbits at 1s. 2d. a lb!

The Town and Country Planning Act of 1947 brought a lot more work, and the firm set up a Commercial Agency to produce advice on planning and development, particularly in the Broadmead area. One of their more unusual tasks was to clear the medieval plague pit on the site where John Lewis now stands, and ensure that the remains were decently buried.

9 – Travelling hopefully.

Part of Bristol's great success as a trading city rested on its communications system – as it still does today. The port opened up trade to South Wales, London, France and the Mediterranean, and eventually the colonies, but the imports arriving at the docks had to be sent on by road. So by the 16th century a network of delivery wagons covered most of the routes in the south of England and South Wales, a fact that all visitors to the city remarked on. Defoe in the 1720s noted the great inland trade: "The merchants maintain carriers, just as the London tradesmen do." The cutting of canals in the 18th century made the network of deliveries even more complex, so that goods could be sent up to Gloucester and then on to the Midlands and the North; and the coming of the railways opened up the market even further, until competition from more modern ports began to have its effect.

As early as 1440, Bristol merchants were using wagons and packmen to deliver their goods; by the 18th century, the network was quite sophisticated, with connecting delivery services designed to cross at fixed points, so that the whole country could be covered. *Mathews' Directory* for 1793 lists 18 daily departures for wagons going all over the country, including Scotland, Ireland and Wales, together with 27 different coach services for passengers, and coasters for 35 different destinations.

The importance of the halliers, as the carriers were called, in Bristol, is demonstrated by the fact that until the 19th century they had their own street, Halliers' Row, the modern Nelson Street. As well as the professional carriers' services, most major merchants operated their own service, and would take passengers as well as goods, so that by the coming of the railways, the range of services was amazing, even if the journeys were slow and the roads unspeakable. By 1837 there were 22 coaches running daily between Bristol and London, and 27 others passed between Bristol and Bath every 24 hours. This was a faster alternative to water transport; in the 1830s, a Bristol linen draper complained that owing to changes of fashion, his goods suffered a 20 per cent depreciation while travelling to London by barge.

There must have been a certain distrust of the railways at first, for Mathews in 1843 lists 22 coaches, 54 stage coaches, as well as wagons, omnibuses and carriages, running from seven coaching inns, and he lists the names of 177 carriers. All this was apart from "land carriages" to all parts of the country, run in conjunction with the railways. For public transport, there was a fleet of hackney coaches, annually licensed and numbered, which plied from 9 a.m. to 11 p.m. at fixed fares per distance and time. This was transport for well-off Bristolians; the poor walked.

What is surprising is that when the railways came, the carriers did not go out of business, but adapted. They used a great deal of ingenuity to integrate their road service with rail and canal links and **Knee Bros,** of Boyce's Avenue, Clifton, actually invented the first-ever container: a road van that could be detached from its wheels and loaded on to a flatbed railway truck.

That was in 1844, five years after William Knee had started a removals business at 26, Temple Street. He became famous for his container wagon, which in 1847, began to travel on the Bristol and Exeter Railway. His sons took over, and they, too, were

Above: Davey's modern Foden steam wagon could travel at an amazing five mph and pull eight tons of goods.

Below: The world's first container van, invented by William Knee in 1844 for removing goods by cart and then rail.

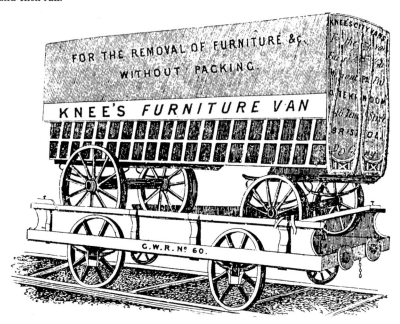

innovators with their pantechnicon, which they showed off in 1912. (At first a pantechnicon was the name for a warehouse, not a van.)

Albert Knee had built up the Temple Street depot into a huge warehouse, with space not just for furniture storage, but for agricultural equipment, and even for storage of the first Bristol aeroplanes, while they awaited buyers. The old railway container wagon, designed in 1844, was still going strong in 1912, alongside steam traction wagons and modern motor vans, and the firm was the first ever to send their vans on railway trucks through the Severn tunnel.

Albert Knee's son Edward joined the firm at the age of 14, when an auction room and an estate agency had been added. In 1970, the Temple Street warehouses were compulsorily purchased to make way for the new fire station, and Knees moved to one of the most interesting Victorian buildings in Bristol, King's Arcade, designed by the self-taught architect and eccentric W.J. King in 1878 as a bazaar and winter garden. The enterprise was unsuccessful, and over the century the building was gradually altered and the garden built on. The building is a real museum piece: a Victorian shopping arcade on three floors, with internal balconies, walkways, and alcoves originally designed for individual shops. At the entrance is a grand staircase with a rose window at the top. After their move to Clifton, the removals side of the business slowed down, and the firm is now mainly a depository.

Many of the firms which now trade as estate agents and auctioneers had more diverse operations in Victorian times. They were also land agents, surveyors, rent collectors and removers and hauliers, as was the firm of **Davey and Co (Bristol) Ltd.** It was launched by Ephraim Davey in 1846, and he, too, was a pioneer in the design of road and rail vans. From horse and cart they went on to railway vans, Foden Steam Wagons which went along at five miles an hour, each with a trailer that could carry eight tons. They had a train of 15 rail wagons and a fleet of huge pantechnicons.

In the 1890s, Davey's were granted Royal Letters Patent for "improvements in vehicles for removing furniture"; their Royal Patent Vans were supplied to the removals trade all over Britain, and also ran on Irish, French, Italian and German railways. They also invented something called Parisian Furniture Polish, and boasted that "carpets brought for cleaning are beaten by the latest improved steam machinery."

The third generation of the family disposed of the removals side of the business to Pickfords after the Second World War, and from then on the business concentrated on estate agency and auctioneering. As early as 1906, Davey's were printing a register of properties for sale on a give-away sheet.

There are unsubstantiated claims that **Pickfords** were established in the city in 1646. This is unlikely since the firm did not really get going until the 18th century, in the North. But they were certainly in Bristol in 1835, when they were using not just road links but waterways as well. Their warehouse was at Stone Bridge, Quay Head, and in 1845 they were advertising that "a wagon for Gloucester every afternoon meets the Railway train to Birmingham, Manchester, Liverpool and all parts of the North", showing that they integrated their delivery services with other forms of transport. By 1865 Pickfords was agent to all the major railway companies up to Scotland, to all ports, to Dublin and to and from any part of France. They also had a fleet of barges.

As horse-drawn buses began to take some of the trade from carriers, who delivered people as well as goods, the firm turned more, in the second half of the 19th century, to removals. The Bristol regional office still has letters (many of them with black borders, showing that a bereavement had caused the move) expressing gratitude for the way the staff had handled the operation: "Not a single article rubbed or defaced, and no breakages." The bill was 4 guineas for a removal from Wolverhampton to Bristol, in 1897.

Carriers apart, the need for a public transport system in the Victorian city became obvious. The railways and cabs carried some of the population, and there were private horse omnibuses, but the huge population increase meant that a proper system, covering more of the city and the suburbs, was badly needed. It took a long time to arrive: the first horse-drawn tramway line, from the King David Inn, Perry Road, to St. John's Church, Whiteladies Road, opened in 1875, run by the **Bristol Tramways Company Ltd.,** ancestor of the modern City and Badger lines.

The *Western Daily Press* described the opening run: "Each car was drawn by four splendid horses in new harness. The uniform of the drivers and conductors is of a greyish colour with scarlet trimmings. Everything being ready, the whistle was sounded and the cars started their journey....all along the route crowds of people were assembled, and as the cars went by, hearty cheers were offered."

By 1880 there were seven tram routes and, at the end of that year, the horses had pulled the trams 500,873 miles and carried over three and a half million passengers. The trams were a great success, and changed Bristolians' lives. The tram routes dictated a new pattern of shopping, for the inhabitants of the big new suburbs could now catch a tram to the old shopping centre in the heart of the city. From this point on, the ambitious shop-keeper aimed to move nearer the centre of the city, and the pressure for sites encouraged the non-retail traders to sell what had become valuable property and move out to the suburbs, a pattern that continues to this day.

The trams also had the important effect of making the population more mobile: workers could take jobs further afield, and this in turn encouraged them to move out to the suburbs without feeling cut off; the trams enabled parents to send their children to schools further away, and they opened up many new areas for leisure and recreation.

But Bristol Tramways did not stop at trams; they hoped to monopolise the public transport system, and by 1886 they also owned 99 hansom cabs, 56 brakes, nine omnibuses, 38 wagonettes – and 50 wheelchairs! They tried out the first steam carriage in 1880, using horse buses instead of trams, and they also ran a funeral bus. The Bristol Cab Company with its distinctive livery, blue with red wheels and its drivers wearing white top hats, started in 1886.

Thanks to Sir James Clifton Robinson, pioneer of electric traction, Bristol was one of the first cities to have electric tramways; electrification was complete by 1900, and in 1901 some of the horses were sold. But there was another rival, the motor bus, which made its first appearance in 1906. These were run in addition to trams, and were hired out for excursions, so that, before the First World War, the Tramways company was offering such diverse services as driving lessons and riding instruction. The famous Blue Taxis were launched, charabancs were built in the city from 1908 onwards and, by 1913, the Tramways Company owned 225 trams, 42 charabancs, 230 taxis and 150 horses. The tramcars and charabancs alone carried one and a half million passengers a week.

A very early photograph of the Pickfords warehouse, on Colston Avenue, before the waterway was covered over. Pickfords were pioneers in using waterways for carrying goods.

Those who could afford it could travel in style in this 1890s brougham & pair, run by the Bristol Carriage Company, who had their stables next to the Greyhound Hotel, Broadmead.

By the Thirties there was a network of motor bus services in the entire region, and the bus was beginning to oust the tram. In 1927, Bristol Tramways started running four super-de-luxe buffet coaches from Bristol to London. The coaches were divided into three sections: the front had 18 non-smokers' seats, in leather with folding tables, and the rear section had eight similar seats for smokers. The centre section had a toilet compartment, a steward's pantry where tea and snacks could be made, and there was a 20 gallon water tank on the roof. The conductor was the buffet attendant and could be summoned by an electric bell.

This kind of service signalled the end for the trams; the last one ran on July 17th, 1939, and the same crowds that flocked to see the service begin came to see the final journey. (In fact, 66 trams were reprieved because of the war, and they ran until 1941). The famous Blue Cabs had come to an end in 1930, when they were sold off for as little as £4 each. From the Second World War on, it was the age of the bus.

When the motor car took over from the horse, it brought the end of several other trades: blacksmiths, livery stables, wheelwrights and cart-makers, corn chandlers and nearly all the harness makers and saddlers disappeared, too.

Only one Bristol saddler and harness maker survived the changeover, **H.A. Matthews and Son,** now of Keynsham. Frederick Matthews set up in Redcliff Street in 1882, making saddles and harness for the hauliers, the railways, Bristol Police and the Corporation, and they also worked for the Wills and Smythe estates. When the telegraph and telephone arrived, they made safety harnesses for the men who had to climb the poles, and in the First World War, the firm supplied the Army, employing 20 harness-makers.

By the Twenties, the motor car was affecting trade, so the family went into haulage as well, taking a whole day to haul beer from George's Brewery from Bristol to Bridgwater. Next came a Model T lorry, used for fetching and delivering to sheep fairs.

Nowadays the business is mainly agricultural equipment, though saddles are still part of the stock. The changeover to agricultural equipment is a neat illustration of the kind of crisis that could happen in the Depression of the Thirties. Frederick's son Harold went to a man who owed the firm a very large sum for harnesses. The man said he couldn't pay – but in his garden were lots of wheelbarrows, shovels, bales of wire and gates. So Harold took them in payment. When he arrived home, his father asked: "What's all this? We're not agricultural merchants." And his son replied: "We are now!"

With shipping, Bristol's other transport system, the story starts much earlier. Long before there was a proper network of roads, Bristol merchants would send their goods by sea to London, Wales or the North. Hotwell water went by this route, and it took six weeks to reach London by ship – just as well that the water's chief virtue was that it did not deteriorate in the bottle. Wine was delivered by sea, too. as was timber, and coastal trows were used for passenger transport before the railways came. The merchant ships had always carried some passengers, but the real start of long-distance passenger services came with steam power.

The shipping firms which have survived over a century were founded at a time when

Bristol's port was in crisis. Up to the end of the 18th century, Bristol had been second only to London in its importance, but two factors made it lose out to Liverpool in the 19th century. The first was the greed and dilatoriness of Bristol Corporation, who charged high dues on all cargoes coming in, and who dithered endlessly about improving the facilities. The other factor was the invention of the steamship. When Brunel's s.s. *Great Western* went on its maiden voyage from Kingroad to New York in 1837, the Corporation thought it would notch up another first for Bristol, and with it the monopoly of the trans-Atlantic passenger and cargo trade. But when the *Great Western* came back, it was expected to pay huge dues – and the vessel was so big that she only came down the Avon with great difficulty. As steamships got bigger and heavier, it was evident that Bristol would lose out to Liverpool, whose dues were far lower and whose dock was larger and deeper.

In 1846, **Mark Whitwill,** whose father had promoted the *Great Western,* joined the firm his father had started in 1831, and from 1848 to 1855, Whitwill's ran a regular service of sailing ships from Bristol to New York and Quebec, and from 1852, to Australia as well, carrying passengers and cargo. But from 1842, no steam ships came from America to Bristol; they docked at Liverpool, and there was a gap until 1871 when Mark Whitwill bought the s.s. *Arragon*. With her, he re-opened trade with America, eventually chartering and buying ships which provided a service to New York, Boston, Philadelphia, Baltimore and Montreal.

Because of the difficulties of using Bristol as a port, and the shilly-shallying of the Corporation, Mark Whitwill II became an ardent advocate of "dockisation" as it was called, either by deepening and improving the port itself, and of excavating the Avon's river bed through the Gorge (an impracticable idea because of the rock foundations), or by building a new dock at Avonmouth. In 1868 he was a member of the board of Bristol Port and Channel Company, a private company set up to do what the Corporation failed to carry out.

The Corporation favoured development at Portishead, and eventually was forced to take over the private scheme, a move which led finally to the opening of Avonmouth Docks in 1877, Portishead Dock in 1879 and the Royal Edward Dock in 1908. But it was too late to recover the trade from Liverpool and only the huge imports of Canadian grain at the end of the 19th century kept the port of Bristol in business. Passenger ships continued to do good business, especially with emigrants to the colonies, though the arrival of the aeroplane signalled another decline.

Mark Whitwill remained a prominent figure in Bristol society: he was one of the prime movers in setting up the Hospital for Sick Children, heading an appeal in 1865, and he became its first President when the hospital opened in 1866. For many years a director of Bristol and West Building Society, he was also a promoter of the Severn Tunnel. His son, Mark III, as it were, was a leading figure in the Volunteer Rifles, and the firm went on trading as Whitwill's until 1974, when it merged with another old firm, **James and Hodder,** which was founded in 1852. In 1985, Hodder Whitwill merged with C. Shaw Lovell.

Hodder's was a firm founded in the 1850s by Hartly Hodder, a shipping owner and broker who started in Sharpness, and then moved to Bristol. He was the first to run a screw tug in the 1870s, and when he retired in 1902, his son took over; he was a councillor and an alderman, and in 1923 became the consul for Germany – a post he felt it was politic to drop in 1939. He also was Danish vice-consul, and the King of Denmark made him a Knight of Danborg.

In the Thirties, Hodder's joined forces with another old Bristol shipping firm run by William and Herbert James, and started a travel agency, something rather unusual at that time. It came into being because Eileen Hartly-Hodder, grand-daughter of the founder, taught a drama student who was no good at acting but good at selling, and she had the idea that he would be ideal to head a travel bureau. Despite family argument, she persisted with the idea. The travel agency, in Shirehampton, is still going strong, and is the one part of the original firm that trades independently.

Little more is known of the early history of the firm because their head office in Queen Square was bombed during the last war, and all records were lost. The family had a distinguished war record, with a DSO, a DSC and an MBE between them. After two Hodder brothers died, their mother took charge of the firm, followed by her daughter, Eileen Hartly-Hodder, who already had a career as a teacher of speech and drama. She found it difficult to cope with both jobs, though she successfully chartered ships, engaged seamen as crews, and arranged passages to countries all over the world. In 1974, she sold out to **C.J. King & Sons**.

Christopher John King set up in Prince Street in 1850 in what was then only just being recognised as a distinct trade, stevedoring. Until then, ships' crews often discharged the cargoes themselves, but as the size of ships entering Bristol increased, stevedoring crews became the rule, unloading cargoes of wine, tobacco and timber, and when at last Avonmouth opened in 1877, C.J., with his son and his brother Samuel, opened an office and played a leading part in developing handling methods and machinery there.

One of his first inventions was The Gadget, a small vessel fitted with a steam winch and carrying rope and tackle which could be attached to the yard-arm of the ship to be discharged. Another first was banana handling: the first banana boat, the s.s. *Port Morant,* arrived at Avonmouth in March, 1901, and C.J. King's unloaded it. In 1907, 56,000 bunches were put on rail from the Elders and Fyffe steamship in only eight hours, when all the unloading was done by hand.

The company was also the first to install at Avonmouth in 1910 two Mitchell floating grain elevators, mechanical devices for transferring grain from ship to shore.

During the Boer War, the cargoes discharged were guns and ammunition, and a decade later there was a mysterious Sunday morning meeting with the military on the Downs, followed by a never-explained embarkation and disembarkation of guns and transport, carefully timed by the watching brass hats. The firm did not know it, but it was a rehearsal for the First World War.

The firm had also invested in tugs, right from the beginning: the first was the *Merrimac,* launched in 1859; it aroused hard feelings, and the tug was threatened by the Pill boatmen who made a living hauling ships bodily down the Avon. *Merrimac's* successor was a paddle driven tug which became well known to Bristolians in the 1880s. When the 44 ton iron paddleboat, the *Gem,* arrived in Bristol on Whit Monday, 1883, citizens were offered a pleasure trip from Hotwells to Chepstow, fare 1s. The *Gem,* launched in 1871, began work in the days of "seeking", which was the privilege of towing windjammers as far out as Land's End, the English Channel and even Bantry Bay. Competition was fierce, and frequently lights would be doused in order to slip out westwards unnoticed by the rival tugs waiting in the darkness. But with this underhand rivalry went a strict ethical code, and once a tug had spoken to her potential customer, the competitors left her severely alone.

The King tugs became famous: two of them escorted the Royal Yacht *Victoria and Albert,* when it arrived in Avonmouth in 1908 for the opening by King Edward VII of the Royal Edward Dock, and one of them worked in the Dardanelles in the First World War. King's was the first firm to operate motor tugs in the Bristol Channel, and when the second war came, they taught the American G.I.'s the art of stevedoring and handled vast amounts of food and petrol and ammunition which came into Avonmouth, while continually under air attack.

Salvage was another function carried out by the tugs; earliest record of one of the King tugs at the scene of an accident was in 1878, when the s.s. *Gipsy* ran aground at Black Rock Quarry, just past the Suspension Bridge, and broke her back. In the Great Fog of 1929, five large vessels ran aground in the Avon, but by the following afternoon, thanks to the tugs, the river was clear and back to normal.

With the decline in shipping in recent years, King's has had to diversify, and one of their present subsidiaries is a joinery business which found a new role in the Falklands War, making transoms, decks and keels for assault craft. The firm closed its stevedoring operation in the Port of Bristol, after 131 years, and the tug company merged with another firm in 1983.

Other nautical trades grew up to support the shipping industry, the oldest of them being ships' chandlering. **John Tratman** opened his business in 1812 in Thunderbolt Lane, Bristol's shortest street, a narrow lane between Prince Street and Narrow Quay. He styled himself ships' provider and sailmaker. By the 1840s he had branched out into paints and varnishes as well, and was wealthy enough to buy shares in ships that were being commissioned; he married one of the daughters of John Edwards, founder of the wine shipping firm Turner Edwards.

He also moved his shop to the end of Narrow Quay where he had room to set up a tinsmith and blacksmith's shop and a sail loft. By the 1880s, his two sons were running the business, and, at the end of the '14-'18 War, E.C. Lowther joined as a partner. Lowther was a master mariner, and his purchase of half the shares enabled the firm to move to the shop on Broad Quay, famous later on for its neon capstan advertisement. The shop was an appropriate purchase, for it had once been a mission for seamen. Lowther's function was mainly contacting and entertaining the visiting captains to the port, and one of the main customers in the Twenties and Thirties was Elder and Fyffes, whose banana boats were supplied to such an extent that Tratman and Lowther opened a branch in Swansea especially to provide chandlery for this customer.

The changeover from sail to steam made a big difference: the sail loft was used to make items for pleasure trips; awnings, boat covers, hatch tents and tarpaulins, instead of the massive sails for clippers and schooners. They also had a rigging department where all the ropes and wires were hand-spliced, while the tinware department produced an incredible range of marine hardware, including pots and pans, lifeboat tanks, metal chimneys, rail-guards and cowls. A permanent occupation for one tinsmith was the renewal or replacement of the glasses in navigation lights.

During the years between the wars, Tratmans continued to thrive, and they purchased a motor vehicle to do the run to Avonmouth to deliver ships' stores; previously they had delivered with a handcart. During the Second World War they supplied the Merchant Navy, and the sail loft made canvas items for the frigates being built by Charles Hill at Albion Dockyard; they also repaired damaged warships. They bought the house next-door in Broad Quay during the war, only to have it blitzed .

The war over, Tratman and Lowther faced huge changes, because oil was taking over from coal and the steam-powered coal barges which they supplied disappeared; the barges had provided their main business.

Another factor that affected them was the trend towards mass-produced chandlery and the decline in the use of canvas. In 1950 they changed course and went into the yacht chandlery business, spotting a growing leisure market. They bought a quantity of Royal Navy surplus stock, and started selling dinghies, making the sails for them in the old sail loft. They also branched out into the domestic paint and wallpaper business, foreseeing a boom in DIY. The new formula was a winner, master-minded by John Tratman III, who died in 1952. The firm was later taken over by C.J. King & Sons who eventually sold out to Ladyline in 1986.

10 – Bristol's Satanic Mills.

The factories of the Industrial Revolution have a hellish image of exploitation and cruelty, but the major surviving Bristol factories escaped this reputation: in fact, the workers who found jobs at Wills, Robinsons, Mardons and Frys were considered the aristocrats of the working class.

The reason must have been that the founders of these enterprises were all Non-Conformists, who saw it as their spiritual and moral duty to treat their employees well, in return for honest labour. To modern taste their attitudes may seem paternalistic, but for their time they were model employers.

Fry's, established by Walter Churchman in 1728, is the oldest chocolate firm in Britain and probably the world. He took out a patent " for the sole use of an Engine for expeditious, fine and clean making of chocolate in greater perfection," and ran his business in Broadmead. In 1761 Joseph Fry, an apothecary, took over Churchman's firm, and in 1777 moved to Union Street. He also had interests in Champion's china works, in a soap works and a Battersea chemicals firm, and ran a type foundry. His wife Anna and his son Joseph took over when he died, and the Union Street factory developed from the Fry home into a huge redbrick empire which was only demolished in 1932, by which time Fry's had transferred to its present home in Somerdale.

What Fry and his son were producing at first was cocoa, not chocolate, which was a luxury not developed until the 1860s; cocoa was sold very much on its health-giving qualities.

Employees at Fry's were expected to be teetotal, Christian, punctual and clean. In return they were given light airy premises and clean working clothes, had a schoolroom and a chapel, and worked for what were in 1866, when an Inspector visited the city, short hours. Girls worked from 8 a.m. to 6 p.m. and men from 6 a.m. to 6 p.m. The inspector found terrible conditions in other places, but he remarked that at Fry's – where 200 people, mainly girls and women, worked – great care was taken over health and education.

In the 1860s there was a system of bonuses for punctuality and fines for lateness; those caught singing, eating the firm's goods, entering beershops in working hours, or acting with any impropriety were subject to censure. Three quarters of an hour after work began, a bell would ring as signal for all the staff to assemble for a morning service; men and women were strictly segregated, and their music while they worked was hymns.

Being strict but kind worked: the firm opened seven new factories in Bristol between 1860 and 1907, and in 1918 Fry's merged with Cadbury's; in 1935 they became a subsidiary, and they are now known as Cadbury-Schweppes; the last of the Fry family associated with the firm died in 1952. During both world wars, millions of Fry's chocolate bars comforted the troops.

Henry Overton Wills, son of a Salisbury clockmaker, came to Bristol in 1786 to join Samuel Wilkinson's tobacco business in Castle Street, at a time when there were 14 tobacco manufacturers in the city.

He started his firm with eight workers, and, typically, used to invite them to dinner, four at a time, on alternate Sundays. This was the first of many benevolent acts that set the Wills employees apart as extra fortunate. H.O. joined forces with Peter Lilley in 1791 at 112, Redcliff Street, and in 1830 his sons, W.D. and H.O., took over. These brothers were very religious, and members of the Penn Street Tabernacle, and they required their employees to be members of a Sunday School – and both brothers were non-smokers! When Luke Thomas left their service in 1837, after 41 years, they had the idea of having his portrait painted, and started a tradition that persisted.

Famous brand names, and the advertising of them, began in the 1840s with Wills Best, Birds Eye and Bishop Blaze Shag, all pipe tobaccos. The next generation of the family, William Henry, joined the firm, at the age of 17, in 1847, and had the job of going around in a dog-cart getting orders.

The American Civil War caused a slump in business in the early 1860s, but W. O. II, asked if he would have to get rid of some of his workers, replied: " I can't do that. These men have wives and children to support. I'll pawn my shirt first."

It wasn't all work at the factory. In 1851, a party of 120 employees went by horse bus and train to the Great Exhibition in London, each with a sovereign in his pocket.

By 1855 there were 16 different types of tobacco being sold, with names like Negro's Head, Bogie Roll and Bright Red Rag. Cigarettes did not become fashionable until the troops discovered them during the Crimean War, and the first that Wills produced were the Bristol brand in 1871, followed by Passing Cloud, Three Castles, Gold Flake and the most famous of them all, Wild Woodbines," five for a penny in a paper packet". In 1883, Harry Wills, grandson of the founder and an engineer, acquired the British patent of the American Bonsack cigarette-making machine that produced 200 a minute, so that in eight minutes, the operative could produce the 1500 cigarettes that had formerly taken all day to make by hand.

Wills was a comparatively happy place to work in, as a report of 1883 shows: "Looking at these trim and tidy girls with smiling faces and nimble fingers, one somehow instinctively feels that the system adopted must have a wonderful influence, for these are as far removed from the Midland and Northern factory hands as can be imagined. The arrangements for the comfort and convenience of the workpeople shows the thoughtful concern that Messrs. Wills have for them. On the various landings there are lavatories and a dressing room, for both men and women, and a library to which all have access".

All this was before Wills moved to their new, modern premises in East Street, Bedminster in 1886, when there was an opening party for 900 staff, with 600 electric light bulbs decorating the building. These premises by 1908 had spread further down the street. The Wills "ladies" who joined the staff, after suitable Sunday school references and a sewing test for dexterity, had to sign indentures which promised that they would "not contract Matrimony within the said term, or play at Cards or Dice." Apprentices then earned 2s. a week for the first year, rising to 6s. a week in the fifth year. But a perk was the annual outing – in 1887 it was to Minehead, with a large van laden with joints and poultry, pies and puddings, strawberries and cream, all prepared in a camp kitchen, and needing 2,000 knives and forks and 40 waiters to serve.

In 1891, the girls' wages went up and the hours were reduced to 8 a.m. to 6 p.m. with one week's paid holiday. By 1893, Wills had its own fire brigade, a brass band, a convalescent home at Clevedon, a library, a savings bank and a dining room which could seat 1,000 and which offered a hot meal with two vegetables for 4d, and three cups of tea or coffee for a penny.

In 1901 Wills, together with the two other large surviving tobacco firms in the city, became founder members of Imperial Tobacco, a group formed to combat the American Tobacco Company which wanted to extend its influence to Britain. Their take-over was fought with the slogan: We'll not encourage Yankee bluff, we'll support John Bull with every puff." Imperial lasted until 1986 when it was taken over by the Hanson Trust, and the East Street operation came to an end in 1975, when the move to Hartcliffe was completed.

Mardons began in 1823 when a John Prince opened a small engraving business at 12, John Street; in 1827 he took on a John Harris, who in 1846 invited his brother-in-law James Mardon to join him in the business, which was by then in Broad Street. The entire plant consisted of three hand-presses, and all the type- setting was done outside. They printed pin papers, address cards and billheads, and one significant order was from Franklins, the tobacco firm, for printed wrappers for tobacco. In 1849, when lithography was in its infancy, James Mardon had the foresight to buy two lithographic presses, and the firm also entered the paper stationery trade. In 1853, one of their apprentices was a certain Walter Vansittart Bowater, founder of the great paper empire.

At about this time the firm took the unheard-of step in the printing industry of giving their employees a half-holiday on Saturdays. By 1859, the firm had grown big enough to move to larger premises in St. Stephen's Street, and the first letterpress machine was installed, so that Mardons could describe themselves on their letterheads as Engravers, Lithographers and General Printers by Steam Power. An "elephant boiler" and a small beam engine supplied the power, and more new technology came in after Heber, James's son, went to France to look at the latest printing presses.

The firm really became a factory in 1869, when they moved to a new four-storey building in Milk Street, where they became the first firm in Bristol to make cardboard boxes, a move which transformed their fortunes. In 1884, they had their first order from Wills to print their cigarette packets, and this became their mainstay. Mardons also printed cigarette cards for Wills from the 1890s onwards. There was so much business that Mardons had to move again, to Temple Gate in 1893 and Temple Street in 1897. They had by then become exclusively printers to the tobacco industry and in 1902 became part of Imperial Tobacco. In 1922, another factory, the 11th, was built in St. Anne's, and by the Second World War, there were 5,270 employees. On November 24th, 1940, disaster struck: seven of the factories were completely destroyed and the following year, two more were wiped out. Mardon's war-work was printing 13 million vital war maps for the Ordnance Survey department and making packaging for food packs for the troops. Since the war, the firm has been rebuilding and expanding again, with factory no.19 opened in 1979.

Elisha Smith Robinson was another entrepreneur who set up in business to service other businesses. He had worked for his grandfather in a small village store near Tewkesbury, where he would pack goods into twists of paper. His father ran a paper mill, so Elisha knew the needs of retailers and had the means to supply them. He came

Above left: This is one calendar that E.S. & A. Robinson printed but never sold: the "Scottish soldier" in the picture is Edward VIII but by the time this 1937 calendar had been produced, the King had abdicated.

Above right: Fry's advertisements were so popular that they were reproduced in postcard form.

to Bristol in 1844, and started out with £400 worth of odd-sized pieces of paper which he had to find uses for as wrapping-paper. He made paper bags by hand and sold them to the grocery trade.

In 1846 he moved to Redcliff Street, and two years later took on his brother Alfred, so that the firm became E.S. and A. Robinson. They started producing account books, too, and in 1856 installed lithographic printing machines which enabled them to print their paper bags with advertisements and illustrations and the trader's name. They also started printing trade almanacs, the old equivalent of the trade calendar. The first bag-making machines were bought in 1860, and in 1873, Elisha saw in America a machine that produced a new satchel-shaped bag; he acquired the rights for Britain, and revolutionised the industry.

Elisha was a jovial, kindly man who always walked about with a paper bag in his pocket. At Christmas he would go round his staff, wishing them the compliments of the season and distributing small gifts. He was an enlightened employer; a comment in 1883, two years before his death, was: "wherever we went, we noticed that the hands, both male and female, seemed to be of a superior class, and that they are evidently well satisfied and contented...in the course of a year, every employee has a week's paid holiday, and there is a capital system of time rewards, whereby everyone in the service of the house earning over 10s. a week is entitled to a sovereign at midsummer, 3d. being deducted for each late arrival. This is an excellent and practical method of stimulating punctuality, and this scheme and holidays cost the firm nearly £1,500 per annum."

The second and third generations of the Robinson family extended the business between 1890 and 1903, when nine new buildings went up, and a disastrous fire at Redcliff Street became the opportunity to modernise. In 1912 they opened the Malago factory, which had a recreation ground on the roof, and in summer work started earlier so that sports could be played in the evening at the firm's sports ground. With pride, they announced a 50 hour week and a profit-sharing scheme, an unusual feature before the First World War, and they started providing medical and dental treatment.

The firm gradually became the most important of its kind in Britain, and spread its operations overseas. In 1966 there was a merger with John Dickinsons, the firm which was founded in 1804, and which was the pioneer of modern paper-making; the Dickinson Robinson Group is now Bristol's largest business with holdings in South Africa, Australia, New Zealand, Canada, the USA and Europe. The firm built Bristol's first skyscraper, on the site of their old office by Bristol Bridge, in 1965.

11 – 'The dirtiest great shop I ever saw' *Horace Walpole*

One of the reasons why so many industrial firms in Bristol have survived for so long is their diversity. In cities where all the industries are similar, the failure of one can mean the failure of all, but in Bristol the sheer variety of trades has prevented a wholesale slump.

The diversity began before the Industrial Revolution, which came to Bristol early, well before the last quarter of the 18th century. Bristol had been industrialised since the 12th century, when the first ever soap-making firms were started; there were iron foundries and zinc and copper works from the mid 17th century, as well as pin-making, sugar refining, glass making, shipbuilding and china-making, and the fuel for all these industries was coal, which was on the doorstep. These manufacturers led the way in experimenting in applications of coal for industry, well before the ironmasters of the Midlands did so.

Unlike other cities created by the Industrial Revolution, Bristol had a Georgian boom, and then another post-Industrial Revolution boom in the 1840s, using all the new industrial techniques that had been discovered. Thus Bristol escaped the worst aspects of industrialisation; the city was not swallowed up by smoky factories and sprawling slums. There was, of course, terrible poverty, and Bristol did have its slums, even in the 18th century; and in the 19th, the city had hundreds of small workshops and sweatshops which used child labour: children from the age of eight worked a 12 hour day in the Bedminster Colliery, for 4d. But when inspections of the city were carried out in 1843 by a government commission, they found Bristol a less shocking place for workers than the other big industrial cities. The one big complaint about Bristol, at this time the third most unhealthy city in the country, was the lack of sanitation for the workers.

In one respect, Bristol can claim to be the cradle of the Industrial Revolution. When a housewife in the early 18th century wanted a cast iron cooking pot, she had to buy an expensive imported one, until Bristol blacksmith Abraham Derby learned how to make them at his foundry at Baptist Mills, where in 1702 with a group of Quakers, he had started a brass mill. In 1707 Derby took out a patent for "a way of casting iron bellied pots and other ware in sand only, without loam or clay." Two years later, Derby moved to Coalbrookdale in Staffordshire, where he was the first to use coke for smelting iron, a discovery that virtually started the Industrial Revolution off. It is tempting to think that Derby did some of his experiments with coke in Bristol.

Only two firms in this book have links with Bristol's first Industrial Revolution boom, and one left Bristol in 1933 to trade in Bath. But **Stothert and Pitt,** founded as an ironmongery business in Bath in 1785 by George Stothert, is too important in Bristol's heavy industry story to be left out.

For there was a connection with Coalbrookdale; Stothert married an Ironbridge girl, and was by 1796 supplying Abraham Derby II with castings for his iron foundry. By the turn of the century they were making ornamental ironwork, cast iron footbridges, agricultural machinery, and even exporting to New York. By 1815 there was a separate iron foundry, and in 1836, Henry Stothert, son of the founder, set up his works in Bristol, in

St. Philips, with an eye to getting work from the GWR making locomotive engines.

When the line between Bristol and Bath opened in 1840, one of the four locomotives on it was Arrow, built by Stothert, and it was the first of dozens, made for the GWR, the Bristol and Exeter, the Bristol and Gloucester and the London, Brighton and South Coast railways. Between 1836 and 1852, Stothert built 150 engines. The firm also made steam pumping engines, including those for the draining of Box Tunnel, and in 1844 they started building iron ships. This company went into liquidation in 1879, but another branch of the family had continued in Bristol since George Kelson Stothert had opened his shipbuilding works at Hotwells in 1852. He was a pioneer in iron shipbuilding and marine engineering, and the firm built ships there until 1904.

The winding-down of the business in Hotwells appears to have happened because in 1897 the Merchant Venturers had sold half an acre of the Floating Dock estate. G.K. Stothert did not wish to surrender his rights, so the case went to court, and he lost. From 1909 to 1933, the Hotwells business seems to have been mainly ship-repairing.

Another pre-Industrial Revolution firm which early on found itself supplying ammunition for wars was **Sheldon Bush.**

The popular and well-worn story of William Watts inventing a method of making lead shot via a drunken dream makes a quaint legend, but it is not likely to be true.

He is supposed to have dreamed that his wife was standing on the tower at St. Mary Redcliffe Church, pouring molten lead on him through the holes in a rusty frying pan. Alternative versions have his wife dreaming of this method of making lead shot. It is a nice legend, and it inspired Bristol's answer to McGonagal, John Dix, to write this dreadful rhyme:

> "Mr. Watts very soon a patent got
> So that very soon only himself could make Patent Shot;
> And King George and his son declar'd that they'd not
> Shoot with anything else – and they ordered a lot."

William Watts was admitted a freeman of Bristol in 1772, and set up as a plumber in Redcliff Street. Since Bristol was the centre of lead manufacturing at the time, Watts would probably have known of the problems in producing lead shot. Dropping the molten lead into water was not a new invention – small shot was made this way in the 18th century. What Watts did was to experiment with the height of the drop, and to use Priddy lead, which had a high arsenic content, thus making the lead fall in globules rather than tears or strings. Watts took out a patent for his process in 1782, describing "a method of making smallshot solid throughout, perfectly globular in form, and without the dimples, scratches and imperfections which other shot, heretofore manufactured, usually have on their surface."

Watts prepared his home at Redcliff Hill in 1775, for conversion into a lead shot manufactory, by cutting a hole in the floors, deepening a well in the basement and building a tower on the roof, to give a total drop of 90 feet. This apparently Heath-Robinson arrangement, with little modification, carried on successfully until 1968, when the premises were demolished for road-widening, and an important piece of industrial archaeology was lost.

Despite his success Watts had his problems: the basement tank got flooded when the

Right up until the demolition of the Redcliffe Hill Shot Tower in 1967, Sheldon Bush were making shot in exactly the same way as the inventor of the process, William Watts.

River Avon was at full tide, and his neighbours complained about the smell. Watts retaliated by attacking those neighbours who kept pigs. In 1787, he took a partner, Philip George of the brewing family. George paid £10,000, and the pair made money: they built a shot-tower in London (Dickens describes it in *Household Words*) and made enough profit to tempt Watts into becoming a building speculator, with disastrous results: he went bankrupt building the spectacular foundations for Windsor Terrace in Clifton, at the time of the slump caused by the Napoleonic Wars. Watts named the terrace in honour of George III, who admired his invention.

Philip George took over the leadshot business in 1818, and carried it on until 1848, when he sold out to James Williams, who later sold the business to the present owners, Sheldon Bush. Almost nothing is known about these two, except that they built up a considerable presence in the lead industry. By the 1880s they had a large smelting works at Blackswarth Road, and a sheet and pipe lead works at Cheese Lane, the present home of the company. The firm always conducted their business aggressively, if politely, as this letter of 1837 to a debtor proves: "Your conduct to us is most extraordinary, and permit us to say, unbecoming the tradesman or gentleman, and such as could not fail to raise in our minds a very strong feeling of anger against you."

They don't write letters quite like that at Sheldon Bush now, but they do make lead shot, in a modern tower, in almost exactly the same way as William Watts did. They are the sole survivors of what was once a big lead industry in Bristol.

Of the second wave of the Industrial Revolution in the city, the earliest survivor is **Mark Priest,** the chain makers, now of Sevier Street, St. Paul's. The firm's roots were in the Black Country, where brothers Mark and John Priest were born. About 1830 their father sent them to Bristol to set up a chainmaking business for the port and the shipbuilding industry, and by 1833 they had a forge in Ellbridge Place (Scamps Alley) which ran down to the Frome by Narrow Weir. They lived in Old Market, next door to the 'Stag and Hounds'.

The older brother Mark confined his business to the family craft of chain and anchor forging, while brother John made gates and railings and farm ironwork. Still in partnership, they opened up a larger forge in Leadhouse Lane, St. Philip's, and acquired the chain-testing machines of a company that had closed down. The brothers parted company in the 1850s, and Mark's son came into the chain and anchor business, which then moved to a site in Old Bread Street; by this time they were also selling "saddle ironmongery".

Mark laid out the new works with forges along the rear centre, and the flues were led out to the base of a brickwork tunnel leading to a smoke stack. The testing-machine and pump, still handworked, were installed. The chainmakers used a good quality slack small coal to fire the forges, and on one occasion there was an explosion, caused by banking up the coal in a live fire to cook a dinner. The entire tunnel was wrecked, and a bellows boy was killed.

At this stage the firm had built up a continuous trade with the tobacco and palm oil trades in the West Indies, supplying chains for the plantations' lifting gear; the sugar cane growers also bought Priest's chains, which were despatched in the casks which arrived at the port. A few days before sailing, the Master of the vessel, with First Mate as bodyguard, would come to Old Bread Street to settle the bill in gold.

At the end of the 19th century three of Mark's sons were in the business, and the trade was changing; a Belgian firm had invented an electrical method for welding links for chains, confounding the Priest brothers' prophesy that chain links could never be made by machine. But the business continued with the hand-forged system which had been invented in 1701. (Even in the 19th century, there were still a few outworkers, mainly women and children, who made small linked chains at home, with a forge in the kitchen or shed.)

In 1908, the last member of the family took up the trade, which by then was regulated by Board of Trade and Factory Acts, as chain had become an important piece of war equipment since 1870. In 1942, the firm changed hands, and the last Priest, Mr. Henry, left to start a firm of his own. He is still alive, and says sadly that there is now no-one left in the city making chains by the old traditional hand methods.

The name of Isambard Kingdom Brunel crops up frequently in this book; another firm he helped indirectly was **W.J. Farvis.** William Farvis began as a blacksmith (not a farrier) in Bedminster in 1840. He had come from Taunton to Bristol to do ironwork for the new Temple Meads station which was being built. He moved to nearby Water Lane, and used to met Brunel in 'The Shakespeare' public house, to get his orders and be paid. Family history has it that the association ended when William Farvis got drunk and walked out on a job!

From bits of ironwork for Temple Meads, William and his sons started working for the Bristol shipbuilding industry, by the 1860s having won some repute by making iron funnels so large that they had to be assembled in Victoria Street, stopping all the traffic. One of his sons joined the Army, was sent off to the Crimea, stuck it for three weeks, and deserted. He changed his name to Turner and ran away to America.

The firm has always had a genius for improvisation. Farvis's were always being asked to make gadgets or adapt machinery; in an advertisement for the firm, which in 1880 seemed to have gone into temporary partnership with an ironmonger, they announced that they were "sole makers of an apparatus for simultaneous opening and closing of windows in greenhouses, hospitals, schools and churches."

The present managing director Ross Floyd, son of William Farvis II's daughter, says that improvisation is a family trait, and that he often invents pieces of farm machinery; he still has some of the Victorian tools that his great-great-uncle used. The firm moved to Morley Road, Southville, in the 1970s, and demolition of the Water Lane site revealed the remains of a 16th century house built with ship's beams for joists – possible evidence that Water Lane was in fact once a waterway.

The **McArthur Group** began with an ironfounding business started near Glasgow in the 1770s. The third generation of the family, John McArthur, came to Bristol in 1838 to work for the famous local firm of Acraman's, who have a street named after them in Southville. Acraman's, which was founded in the 18th century, was by the 1830s a big firm, with three Bristol works, where they built bridges and cranes, made anchors and, later, locomotives and iron ships. They helped build the s.s. *Great Western,* and finally had a spectacular bankruptcy in 1842, with debts of £75,000.

Young John McArthur had got out just before the crash, in 1839, and in the next year he started his own business in Charlotte Street, as "iron, copper and tinplate merchant, wholesale ironmonger and maker of edge tools." He later bought some of the Acraman interests, and Britain's railway mania kept him going with demands for his pig iron. In 1846 when Bristol Waterworks was formed, the site of the McArthur edge-tool works at Chew Magna was required for the reservoir, and from then on he stuck to the sale of copper and tin, and gave up their manufacture into tools. He died in 1864, leaving his heirs a fine collection of 22 paintings, some of them by the Bristol school of artists, but all but one were sold at auction, for £8,740.

In a new partnership, his son Donald carried on, and the firm moved to Marsh Street in 1871. Business in Ireland was extended, with the opening of a Dublin office in 1883; the firm is still there. Allan McArthur, the youngest son of the founder, joined in 1887, and three years later they opened an office in London, followed by another in West Bromwich. In 1911 the old Marsh Street warehouse floors had caved in – not surprisingly, considering the weight of the iron stored there – and expensive repairs had to be done; but the firm stayed there until the Second World War, until the Merchants' Hall next door was bombed, and they decided to move to Gas Ferry Road. Over the century, McArthurs had taken over many smaller firms, and by the end of the 1950s, they needed more space, so they moved to their present home in Speedwell. The old McArthurs warehouse is now Artspace, the home of painters and sculptors.

There are still members of the McArthur clan in this now huge concern, one of the largest private family-controlled businesses in the country, with branches all over the United Kingdom and Ireland.

Strachan and Henshaw, founded in 1879 by Robert Price Strachan, an Irishman, and George Henshaw, started in the shadow of the E.S. and A. Robinson factory, which probably explains why right from the beginning, the firm was interested in paper-bag making machines. Both men were apprentices of Hodge, an engineer in Thomas Street and builder of the satchel bag-making machine for Robinsons.

The pair started in a converted house in Long Row, off Victoria Street, making appliances connected with the paper bag and printing trades, and also became efficient general engineers. In 1890 they moved to Lewin's Mead; they needed the space because the old house was so crowded that machinery parts had to be assembled in the street. About this time they developed a rotary stereo printing machine capable of printing paper bags during the process of manufacture, and these machines made them an international reputation: they sold them in Russia, Scandinavia, Italy, Rumania, France, Turkey and Australia.

Strachan and Henshaw also got the contract to install power and power distribution for the great Bristol Industrial Exhibition in St. Augustine's Parade in 1893, and in the 1890s they also got involved in work for the new electric tramways system being set up in the city. This resulted in another contract for tramways work, in South America.

In 1904 the firm moved to its present site at Whitehall, and developed some new lines in goods hoists, water pumps and electric transporters. Then came the war and normal production virtually ceased, because the company became a munitions factory, making shells and gun parts. Girls were taken on for the first time ever, and great care was taken to stagger their shifts with the men's, so that the two sexes never met.

Early in 1920, E.S. and A. Robinson acquired the whole business, and Strachan followed Henshaw into retirement. The new owners stimulated research into more sophisticated colour-printing paper-bag machines, and, just before the Second World War, the firm had great hopes of selling in Russia – they had even printed a catalogue in Russian (by the Thirties, their catalogues were always tri-lingual) – but the Russians never saw them. Other memories of the Thirties include a spirited black horse which pulled the delivery cart, men working by the light of naked gas flames, and a ship's bell that signalled breaks, met with cries of "Smoko!".

But in 1940, once again, the firm went over to war work, which included the development of equipment for field survey units, gun carriages, and launching rigs; they made submarine-detecting apparatus and torpedo parts, fuse machines, anti-aircraft shells, and trench mortar bombs. During the war the firm also made a giant railway-truck tipper, 120 feet tall and so large that neighbours living in Whitehall feared that enemy pilots would use it as a target. The firm had to charter a plane to fly over and take aerial photographs to make sure it was invisible.

Girls had not been allowed to work in the plant between the wars, but they came back again in 1940, and even worked night shifts – once again staggered for propriety's sake! In 1958, the old Central Engineering Works in Lewin's Mead was closed after 68 years; in 1968 came the Queen's Award for Industry, and in 1979 the firm celebrated its centenary with a big day out at Dodington, with a bumper garden party, bands and a centenary mug.

The next survivor is **Llewellin's Machine Co.Ltd.,** which started in a small gas-lit workshop behind King Square in 1883. The frontage was a Georgian house in whose forecourt John Wesley had preached, and the building looks much the same today. The original business centred on the design and production of clockwork time-checking machines. "Clocking-in" clocks were invented in 1885 in America, but Llewellins were not far behind, making them in 1888.

William Maberly Llewellin was an inventor and patent-agent, and his innovative skills were responsible for what is thought to be the first double helical gear cutting machines in Europe. Another product of the early days was the first tangential feed hobbing machine made in this country. In the 1890s the firm was also a bell foundry, making bells for the many Victorian churches being built in the city.

In the First World War Llewellin's was engaged chiefly in machining shell cases for the Ministry of Munitions and in the Second in resisting the effects of German incendiaries which threatened to burn out the business. That time round they made thousands of gears for everything from tanks to aeroplanes.

At the turn of the century, Nos.13 and 14, King Square were acquired and new workshops built at the back. Until 1927 the business had been the sole property of the eccentric and autocratic Mr. Llewellin but that year it became a limited company with him as chairman. Since the last war the firm has taken larger premises in nearby Dighton Street, and the original buildings, which are listed and protected, are only offices. The main product of the company now is gears of all kinds, for anything from food firms to the nuclear industry.

It may seem odd that a firm which sells oil fuel for heating can be well over a century old. **Butler Oil Products Ltd,** of Avonmouth was founded by William Butler in 1843 at the picturesque beauty spot of Crews Hole. He had worked before that on the Bristol

Top of page: Female munitions workers at Strachan &
Henshaw, during World War One. Women had never
worked there before, and then shifts were designed so
that they never saw the male employees!

These magnificent baths, some of them with marble
linings, stood in Gardiner's showroom in the
Edwardian era.

Llewellins of Kings Square besides selling time clocks,
were also bell founders in the 1890s.

and Exeter Railway under Brunel, and came to the city to be manager of a new tar distilling works. The distillation of coal tar was important for its by-products: creosote oil, which Brunel used for preserving railway sleepers, lamp black and pitch, a product which William Butler mixed with small coal to make briquettes, and with gravel to make tarmacadam, named after Bristol road engineer John Loudon Macadam.

Another and most important by-product was Benzole, which led to the creation of synthetic dyes, and of course became motor fuel with the invention of the motor car. By 1903, a Bristol firm was advertising that "a Quadrant Bicycle, ridden daily in Bristol, wet or fine, has been run 177 miles on one gallon of our Highly Rectified Spirit." It sold for 10d. a gallon!

William Butler, a staunch Methodist, was very interested in transport. He was instrumental in the setting up of the Bristol Tramways Company, and was it first chairman – at his death in 1900, when he was lowered into his grave (he built his own family vault) all the trams of Bristol remained stationary for one minute.

At his death, the firm was flourishing: there was a works at Gloucester, which was served by river with six lighters and a steam tug, and the firm also owned four trows for the South Wales trade, as well as a coasting steamer, the *Clifton Grove Special*. Butler's was the first firm in Bristol to try out the telephone, with a privately installed line between their works and head office, set up in 1879. The *Western Daily Press* laboured to explain the new-fangled operation: "There is an electric bell at each end for calling attention and by an ingenious contrivance, a person at the St. Philips side can ring the bell at Crews Hole without sounding the one affixed on the side at which he is engaged, thereby obviating the confusion which is sometimes caused when bells are rung at both ends of the wire....the work is a marvel of simplicity and the whole thing has been constructed at an expense so moderate that one shilling per week will cover the interest on the amount of outlay."

The founder's sons, William and Thomas, also have another claim to fame. They were some of the first men in Bristol to buy motor cars; Thomas Butler obtained the first Motor Licence and had the first registered car in the city. It was a familiar number: AE1, the number that now adorns the Lord Mayor's official car. Thomas Butler's was a splendid 12 HP, 4-cylinder Clement, purchased at the Paris Motor Show in 1904.

In the First World War, Butler's made an important contribution to the war effort, since they were able to produce Benzole and toluene for explosives; they set up the first plant in the country to produce it, and in the process distilled 22 million tons of tar during the war. In the Twenties and Thirties came two more significant derivatives of tar: pyridine, which became a chemical for the drug trade for the making of M and B tablets, and the development of the earliest form of plastic, Bakelite, from tar acids. When the Second World War came, Butler's were again supplying the war effort, with pitch for surfacing aerodromes, creosote for high octane aeroplane fuel, toluene for TNT, and naphthalene for plastics.

Godwin Warren Engineering nowadays make automatic and electronic equipment, but when William Warren started up his business in the 1790s, it was as a wholesale ironmonger at Bridge Street. By 1870, when his son Robert was in charge and when James Godwin became a partner, the firm was making fasteners, fixings and steel. In 1910 they became a private limited company and by 1920 were the largest steel stockists in the region, with their own engineering department to satisfy cut bar demand. Jobbing engineering projects were taken on, and by 1952 they were making electric consoles and panels, steel pit props, and ASDIC equipment for the Royal Navy. Work for the railways followed, friction buffer stops and level crossing barriers; and, endlessly versatile, they started making starting-stalls for horse-racing courses, and car-parking systems. In 1970 they went into computerised parking.

After various changes of ownership, they are now owned by Institutional Investors, and there is now an American subsidiary of the firm which started out on one floor of a house in Bridge Street.

The 19th century ironmongery businesses did not all develop in the same direction, as the story of **Gardiner Sons and Co.** of Broad Plain proves. The firm was started in 1825 by a Zacharias Cartwright, as a builders' and cabinet makers' ironmonger at 11, John Street. Legend has it that he did not disdain to deal in junk as well. When he died, the business was acquired by his nephew Emmanuel Chillcott, who in 1860 took on a partner Alfred Gardiner. He was the son of John Gardiner, founder of Wathen Gardiner and had been sent by his father to Australia to learn business methods. He came home, and expanded Chillcott's little firm into a huge empire.

Alfred's two sons, John and Thomas, joined him in 1871, and in 1874 they bought an ex-boot factory in Nelson Street. Gradually property was bought in All Saints Street and Duck Lane, where they made windows and ironwork and church furnishings, and in 1897 Thomas opened the Midland Ironworks in St. Philips. The Nelson Street and All Saints Street works became so huge that one assistant who had worked for the firm for a year had to ask one of the Gardiners how to find the way back to his department. The firm had representatives travelling by horse and trap all over the West and into Wales.

The Midland Ironworks was supplying shop signs, shop fronts and steel work for building, the ironmongery department fitted out restaurants and hotel kitchens, and there were lighting and gardening departments, as well as a huge range of plumbing and building equipment on sale. In the Boer War, the firm made saddle arches for the cavalry, and in the First World War trench mortars, bombs and aeroplane parts.

In 1930, Gardiner's bought the Queen's Hotel, which had been built in 1854 in Queen's Road, for their main retail showroom. They converted the upstairs bedrooms to offices and rebuilt the old stables, dining room, lounge and cellars as showrooms, making it one of the biggest enterprises of its kind in the country. They renamed it Beacon House.

When the Second World War came, production at the Midland Ironworks changed almost overnight. They made transport boxes for torpedoes, panels for the famous Bailey Bridges and lattice girders for the sea-borne Mulberry harbour. They also built gun mounts, radar mounts, rocket launcher bases and exhaust pipes for the Bristol Aeroplane Company, and, most secret of all, experimental models in copper of the aircraft carrier HMS *Illustrious* and the battle cruiser HMS *London*. So hush-hush was the work that the designers, who were experimenting with flooding valves, had to work under cover of darkness, and the models were taken from the works through a window, so that the employees would not see them.

After the war, Beacon House was sold to Taylor's and then to Jones, both department stores, and in 1958 the firm sold the Nelson Street and All Saints Street

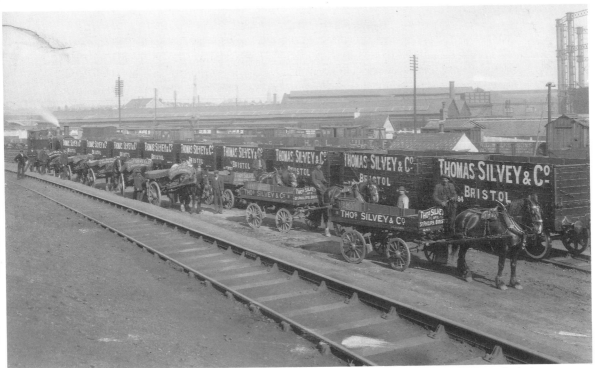

Above: This proud line-up of all the Thomas Silvey coal wagons and carts was photographed at the Midland Road coal yard, circa 1920.

Below: Mr and Mrs Thomas Butler and friends in their 1904 Clement, with the number plate that is now on the Lord Mayor's official car.

works and moved to their present home, the former soap factory. In 1970 they were taken over by Carlton Industries, now part of Hawker Siddeley, and the manufacturing part of the business was discontinued. The builders' merchants side of the firm continued to expand with branches at Cirencester and Shepton Mallet, and Haskins joined the firm on a franchise basis in 1972. The last Gardiner left the firm in the Fifties.

It is just possible that the family dates back to Cabot's time, for a John Gardiner sailed with him to America. Another John Gardiner was Warden of the Merchant Venturers in 1626.

In their early days, many of the firms described in this chapter depended on coal, and some of it was probably delivered by **Thomas Silvey,** from 1870 on. Silvey, who was born in 1839, worked for the Gloucester Railway and Carriage Company, who built railway rolling stock, and he realised that money was being made by the owners of private wagon fleets. As the coal trade was the biggest user of railway wagons, he felt that as a coal merchant he would best be able to use his railway expertise.

Since coal was almost the sole source of energy, Thomas Silvey was soon supplying public utilities, industry and domestic users, and early customers were the gas companies at Bristol, Bath, Bridgwater, Thornbury, Dursley, and most of the Cotswold towns. Similar electrical undertakings bought his coal, and his fleet of wagons was well used. More industrial customers came along, like George's Brewery, St. Anne's Board Mills, Fry's; the bacon curers in Wiltshire and the brickworks of Somerset and Gloucestershire were all supplied via railway sidings, or by road, using horses and carts.

Thomas Silvey's second son Gilbert joined the firm, despite his ambitions to be a banker, and took over in 1900 when his father died. A family row followed. The eldest son Frank, seeing the success of the business, decided to leave his job and join the family firm, but the two brothers did not get on, so Frank left and set up a competing coal business in Fishponds. This business was amalgamated with the original firm nearly 70 years later.

Because many industrial customers were sited on docks in the Bristol Channel, the firm built up a fleet of small sailing colliers carrying coal from the South Wales and Forest of Dean pits. At the end of the First World War, these were replaced by motorships, the first being the m.v. *Nigel,* which had been built as a landing craft for the Gallipoli campaign but never used.

Gilbert Silvey's son Thomas, who is now chairman, joined the family firm in 1930, at a time when it had been made sole agent in the South West for a number of the then privately owned collieries; in 1934, his brother Bryan joined, too. After the war came nationalisation; Silvey's fleet of several hundred railway wagons was taken over, and the firm started investing in towing companies. In 1963, Thomas Silvey II became President of the Coal Merchants' Federation of Great Britain, and became involved with Dr. Beeching, of railway line cuts fame, and Alf Robens, during the negotiations to rationalise the railways – moves which brought tremendous changes for the coal trade.

The old m.v. *Nigel,* still going strong in 1963, was chartered to a developer of the Milford Haven oil refineries, and this pointed to a new direction for the firm, as the coal industry began to shrink. (Nowadays coal accounts for only 10 per cent of the turnover, while oil distribution and a chain of filling stations account for most of the rest.)

In 1964 the *Nigel* was equipped as a sand dredger, and that year was reported in

Lloyds List as adrift in the Irish Sea. A dispute with the charter party followed, and one dark night a crew from Silvey's secretly repossessed her at Milford Haven, and chartered her out to a sand dredging business – and this is how Silvey's got into sand supplying. They are now the eighth largest sand dredging company in the country.

In 1976 the firm moved to Newfoundland Road, and two years later the fourth generation of the family, Thomas Michael Silvey became Managing Director.

12 – In sickness and in health.

In these days of safe drinking water, we tend to forget what dangerous stuff it was right up to 1846, when **Bristol Waterworks** was set up.

The abundance of wine and beer concerns in Bristol up to the 19th century reflected not over-bibulous tendencies, but a fear of local water. Until Bristol Waterworks started piping-in pure supplies, the city relied on a mixture of piped spring water, river water, spa water and rainwater. If you were lucky you had a private well, and firms were still digging wells in the new suburbs such as Redland, right up to the 1870s. A well-owner could sell water to neighbours. In times of drought, householders became desperate, and there was of course no supply of water for sanitation or street cleansing.

There had, in fact, been a Bristol Waterworks Company formed in 1695; it proposed to pipe water from Hanham Mills in elm pipes to the city, but the enterprise never got off the ground. Another wild scheme was launched, in 1811, to dig a canal between Bath and Bristol to provide unfiltered drinking water and a route for barges at the same time!

Meanwhile, in Clifton, locals were making money out of water. The Sion Spring, discovered in the 1780s by boring 250 feet into the rock, produced 33,560 gallons a day, and as well as serving a bath house (now part of the St. Vincent Rocks Hotel), the water was sold at a penny a bucket. Some of the houses in near-by Caledonia Place still have iron traps in the pavement, giving access to water cisterns where they stored the Sion Spring water. By the 1840s, some 400 houses had water piped direct from Sion Spring, and there were other profitable springs in Buckingham Place, Richmond Place and Whiteladies Road. Water-selling was a lucrative trade all over the city, and Bristol Waterworks bought up all these sources for what were then considerable sums: the Sion Spring was sold for £13,500.

Bristol Waterworks' scheme, finally realised in 1847, was to pipe clear water from Somerset across Bedminster Bridge and into the city, thus ending what a government commission called in 1840 "a system obtaining in Bristol of a supply of water from draw-wells or pumps, that engenders filthy habits directly acting upon the health and indirectly upon the morals of the people".

Bristol Waterworks' scheme was preferred to a strange one put forward by the Merchant Venturers, owners of the Hotwell spring, to pump up its by then non-healing waters to a vast reservoir by the Observatory.

Once the city had an adequate supply of clean water, public health improved dramatically and rid Bristol of its reputation as the third most unhealthy city in the country.

If you did fall sick, in the Victorian period, you were more likely to go to a chemist or druggist than a doctor: the Victorians were huge consumers of patent remedies. One of the chemists they would have patronised was **Spracketts,** who now have six branches in the city. The firm was started in the 1840s by George Sprackett, who set up as a dispensing chemist and export druggist, dealing wholesale and retail in patent medicines. He began trading in Wine Street, but since the port played an important part in his trade, moved to Broad Quay in 1864. He made a good living supplying ships' medicine chests – something the firm does to this day – and he used the ships to carry his patent medicines for sale abroad, and thereby built up an export business which continued up to the Second World War.

His son William Haycroft Sprackett took over in the 1870s, and was well-known in the city for being an autocrat. He would arrive at the shop in his carriage and expect the staff to rush out and hold the doors open for him. He was famous for his encounter with a haughty lady customer: "I want a quarter of a pound of brimstone," she said. William Haycroft Sprackett said: "Yes, madam, that will be sixpence." "If I go to Mr. Hodder (a rival chemist) I can get it for fourpence", she complained. "If you go to hell, you can get it for nothing," snapped Mr. Sprackett.

He had no heir, and in the 1920s sold the business to Mr. Ernest Paterson, who can well remember the remedies of the day. "There was my own preparation, Ketts Tablets for Rheumatism, which sold in hundreds and thousands, all over the world, at 1s. 3d. a bottle. We used to make our own cold and influenza mixture of ammoniated quinine, which was very popular with the stars at the Hippodrome. Beechams Pills were sold by the thousand," he remembers. He, too, supplied the ships which, before the last war, were moored literally on his doorstep, and would go to Avonmouth, Cardiff and Newport to fit up the ships' medicine chests according to Board of Trade regulations.

A necessity to us, but a luxury to Victorians, were spectacles. Considering that they read and sewed by candle, oil or gaslight, the need must have been great. But until the beginning of the 19th century, opticians were rare: if you needed lenses you went to a nautical shop which sold telescopes and magnifying glasses and was run by a Mr. Jackson on Bristol Quay in the 1790s. His son-in-law John Braham took over, and by the 1840s had established a wholesale and manufacturing optician's business in London. There, on top of a horse-drawn bus, he met **Matthew Dunscombe** of Bristol, and took him into the firm. After 12 years of study to get certificates in acoustics, light and heat from the "College of Science and Art", Matthew Dunscombe came back to Bristol to take charge of the Braham business, which, in 1874, he purchased. (His original shop was a few doors higher up than the present one on St. Augustine's Parade.)

Spectacles in the Victorian period were a very hit-and-miss affair, depending on the degree of training of the optician, for anyone could set up as one, without qualifications. The selection of lenses was very limited and they were all flat; bi-focals of a crude kind were made by sticking smaller lenses on with glue. But Matthew Dunscombe, who did his own lens grinding, was highly qualified for the time; he wrote many learned articles on vision and was one of the first to produce fused bifocals. By 1900, he had built up a large and unique collection of eyeglasses and spectacles from all over the world; he showed them at the Brussels Exhibition of 1910, only to have them completely destroyed by a fire. He then started another collection, which is now in the South Kensington Science Museum, and his descendants have started a third collection.

Matthew was also interested in photography, and began selling cameras and equipment, with his son Ernest in charge, and his daughter, splendidly named Adeliza Amelia Clara Mary Elizabeth Emma Frances, became the first-ever woman to pass the exams of the British Optical Association in 1899.

By 1910 the photographic business was going strong, and Dunscombes published a monthly booklet called *Photographic Chat;* they also hired out Magic Lantern and Dissolving View Apparatus, and had a library of 20,000 slides. When movies came in,

Dunscombes opened, in 1935, "a miniature Cinematograph Theatre to cater for those interested in home movies", where they showed amateur and professional films, and it is thanks to them that Bristol has a unique colour record of the city in war-time. The firm was able to get hold of some American colour film at a time when only black and white film was available. They also made a film of Bristol at Coronation time in 1953.

The photographic side of the business ended in 1965 when they came to an arrangement with Husbands, trading on the other corner of Denmark Street. Both firms were opticians and photographic dealers, so they compromised: Dunscombes kept to the optical side and Husbands to the photographic.

When the pills and the specs failed, and the end came, there were the funeral directors to turn to.

Before the last war, there were probably around 50 family-owned funeral directors' firms in the city. Now only a handful remain – all the rest have been taken over by the big groups. Funerals were very big business in the 19th century, when Queen Victoria set the fashion for prolonged and deep mourning. The ostentatious funeral was a Victorian invention; in the 18th century, the work would be done either by a carpenter, a mason or a draper, and these three trades are the usual origin of the 19th century firms.

Thomas Pakeman was a draper before he started his funeral firm in Whiteladies Road in 1870; he had supplied mourning clothes as a sideline. Mourning wear was big business, since the whole family, and their servants, went into black for specified periods, according to the degree of kinship. Bristol had two funeral warehouses selling mourning clothes, and dyers advertised "black dyed every week".

One of the oldest surviving funeral firms seems to be **Cotton and Sons** of Eastville, who were founded around 1855 by Alonzo Cotton, a tinsmith, in West Street, Old Market. He deserves fame for another reason: in 1877, his wife fell down the stairs, and, to get her to the BRI, Alonzo Cotton naturally used his horse and funeral cart – and in so doing introduced the idea of starting a branch of St. John's Ambulance Brigade in the city. He hired out his horse and cart to them and eventually became their Chief Superintendent, and won the MBE. He was succeeded by his sons George and Lionel, who exchanged horses and plumes for a motor hearse in 1926, and the business was then handed down to the present owner, another Alonzo, whose son Michael is also in the firm.

Thomas Davis was a Bristol orphan who was taken under the wing of Thomas Bishop, who ran a carriage and fly hire service, as well as a funeral business, in Bedminster. Thomas Davis was apprenticed and himself took over the business in 1870. The firm's ledgers, which date back to 1846, show the high mortality rate in Bristol in page after page of child deaths and adult deaths under the age of 30. Davis and his sons after him provided all the pomp of a Victorian funeral, with horses and mutes, and black ostrich feathers, right up to 1946, when the founder's grandson, Brian, reckons they held the last old style horse-drawn funeral in the city. He says they still get the odd request for horse-drawn funerals and have to hire the coach and horses from Dodington.

119

Above: Thomas Davis Ltd's first funeral car, a 1927 sleeve-valve Daimler Laundalette, bought second-hand from the Earl of Ducie for £500. Pictured outside Ashton Court.

Below: The stonemason's yard behind Bedminster Parade, where Burnell Tovey's funeral firm was established in 1860.

A monumental mason who started up in business in 1860 was **Edwin Burnell,** who had a yard in East Street, Bedminster, site of the firm to this day. He was a monumental mason until 1914, when his son-in-law Albert Tovey started doing funerals as well. Their very first was for a Mrs. Spratt, in 1914; they provided "a polished elm coffin, brassed fittings, brocade padded sides, flannel robe, inscription, plate and bearer, one no.3 car and one no.2 carriage, all for £7. 2s. – and the bill was never paid! "Well", said Albert philosophically to his son Reginald, "that was the Spratt to catch a mackerel."

The fifth Burnell-Tovey, as the business became styled, is Richard, who reckons he is the best qualified funeral director in the land, with a B.Sc, an M.Sc, and Dip F.D. – and he says he never intended to go into the business!

His great-great-grandfather has another claim to fame: he was a highly religious man who founded the East Street Baptist Church; the first Bible classes were held above what is now the funeral parlour.

The austerity during and after the Second World War, put an end to the extravagant funeral with mutes, velvet pall, cloaks and child attendants, and mourners gave up wearing black for months and writing on black-edged writing paper and carrying black-edged handkerchiefs. The only vestiges of long-term mourning that we retain are the black tie and armband, a relic of the crepe bands that Victorian Bristolians wore on their hats. Even in their passing, Bristol's famous traders liked to have everything ship-shape and Bristol fashion.

Bibliography

Annals of Bristol, John Latimer
The City and County of Bristol, B. Little, 1954.
The Merchant Venturers of Bristol, P. McGrath.
The History of the Antiquities of Bristol, W. Barrett.
Bristol: An Architectural History, Gomme, Jenner and Little, 1979.
The People's Carriage, Bristol Omnibus Co. Ltd. 1874 – 1974.
Shops and Shopping, Alison Adburgham, 1964.
Nation of Shopkeepers, Greville Havenhand, 1970.
Bristol and the Wine Trade, Anne Crawford, 1984.
Printing in Bristol, A.P. Woolrich, 1984.
William Worcestre's Itineraries, J.H. Harvey, 1969.
A Tour through England and Wales, Daniel Defoe, vol 2.
Leisure in the Changing City, H.F. Meller, 1976.
The Bristol Waterworks Co., F.C. Jones, 1946.
Bristol Observed, J.H. Bettey, 1986.
Bristol's Other History, Bristol Broadsides, 1983.
A History of Shopping, Dorothy Davis, 1966.
Victorian and Edwardian Shop-workers, W. Whitakker, 1973.
The Rise and Progress of Industrial Co-operation in Bristol, E. Jackson.
Reminiscences of an Old Draper, W.H. Ablett, 1876.
Chronicle of Bristol, W. Adams.
Ports of the Bristol Channel, 1893.
Public Health in Mid-Victorian Bristol, D. Large and F. Round.
Victorians Unbuttoned, Sara Levitt, 1986.
Hotheads and Heroes, The Bristol Riots, 1831, Peter Macdonald, 1986.
Traffic and Transport, G.L. Turnbull, 1979.
Mathew's and Wright's Street Directories.
Morgan's Guide, 1850; Hunt's Guide, 1850.

LIST OF FIRMS

The references are to the pages on which the main profile of each firm appears. In many cases there are other references in other parts of the book.

Alexandra Workwear 38
Allen, Davies & Co 76
Arrowsmith, J.W., 78
Averys of Bristol 29

Baker Baker & Co 37
Beer, Alfred, 53
Bell, Joseph, & Son 50
Bevan Hancock & Co [now Bevan Ashford] 82
Bristol & District Co-operative Society 17
Bristol & West Building Society 46
Bristol Law Society 81
Bristol Tramways Co Ltd [later Bristol Omnibus Co Ltd] 92
Bristol United Breweries 33
Bristol Waterworks Company 117
Britton, G.B., 41
Brokenbrow, William 21
Bromhead (Bristol) 63
Brooks Service Group 44
Burges Salmon 82
Butler Oil Products 110

Cartwrights 83
Cattybrook Brick Works [now Ibstock Brick] 54
Chillcott, Alfred, & Co 66
Clarks Wood Co 51
Collard, A.D., 25
Collins, Thomas, & Co 24
Cordeux's 36
Cotton & Sons 119
Courage's 33
Cowlin, William, & Son 48
Crispin, James, & Sons 22
Curtis, Jenkins, Cornwell & Co [now part of Coopers & Lybrand] 85

Davey & Co 91
Davis, Thomas, 119
DRG [Robinsons] 101
Duck, Son & Pinker 61
Dunscombe, M.W., 118

Elworthy, George S., & Co 76
Evangelical Christian Literature, Bookshop 74

Farvis, W.J., & Sons 108
Ford & Canning 12
Frost & Reed 65
Fry's [now Cadbury-Schweppes] 99

Gardiner Sons & Co 113
George's Booksellers 74
George's Brewery 33
Gibbs, George, 69
Godwin Warren Engineering 112
Grace, Darbyshire & Todd [now part of KMG Thomson McLintock] 85
Grand Hotel (the) 68

Hall, John [now Berger Decorative Paints] 50
Harris, Alfred, 79
Harvey, John, & Sons 30
Hill, Jonathan [now Wickham Norris] 51
Hoddell Pritchard 55
Hole, C.J. 59
Howells of Bristol 31
Husbands & Sons 61

James and Hodder [now C. Shaw Lovell] 95
Jollys [now House of Fraser] 37
Jones [now Debenhams] 37

Kemp, W.W., & Son 68
King, C.J., & Sons 96
Knee Bros 89

Lalonde Bros & Parham 57
Latchams, Montague, Niblett & Co 81
Lennards 42
Lenton, J., & Sons 24
Llewellin's Machine Co 110
Lloyd Bros (Bristol) 18

Mardon Son & Hall 101
Marsh, T.C., & Son 40
Matthews, H.A., & Son 94
May & Hassell 53
McArthur Group 108
Mogford, W.H., & Son 49

Osborne Clarke 81
Osmond Tricks 55

Pakeman, Thomas, & Son 119
Parker, Edward T. 59
Parnall & Sons 11
Parsons the Jewellers 66
Perkins, John, & Son 48
Phillips, J.R., & Co [now Allied Lyons & Whitbread] 27
Pickfords Removals 91
Prestridge's 79
Priest, Mark, & Sons 107
Purimachos 46

Rawlings & Son (Bristol) 32
Robbins 54
Roberts Bros (Bristol) 22
Ross, W. & A. 84
Robinson, E.S. & A., 101

St Vincent Rocks Hotel 69
Sheldon Bush & Patent Shot Co 105
Silvey Group 115
Smele & Son (Bristol) 23
Smith, W.H., & Son 79
Solomon Hare & Co 86
SPCK, Bookshop 74
Spracketts 117
Steer & Geary [now Bedford, Steer & Geary] 40
Stock Beech & Co 87
Stothert & Pitt 104
Strachan Henshaw Machinery 109
Stubert Sporrts Wear 44
Sturge, J.P., & Sons 87
Sully, J. & A.W., & Co 85

Tovey, Burnell, 121
Tratman's Ladyline [Tratman & Lowther] 97
Tribe Clark [now Deloittes, Haskins & Sells] 84
Turner Edwards & Co 31

Veals Fishing Tackle 71

Ware, Thomas, & Sons 41
Wasbroughs 83
Wathen, Gardiner & Co 35
Western Daily Press [now BUP] 72
Whitwill's [now C. Shaw Lovell & Sons] 95
Williams, John H. 23
Wills, W.D. & H.O. 99
Wise, T.J., & Co 25
Wright, John [now part of The Institute of Physics] 76